ABOVE
THE BOARD

ABOVE THE BOARD

HOW ETHICAL CEOs CREATE HONEST CORPORATIONS

PATRIZIA PORRINI, PH.D.
LORENE HIRIS, D.P.S.
GINA PONCINI, PH.D.

New York   Chicago   San Francisco   Lisbon   London   Madrid   Mexico City
Milan   New Delhi   San Juan   Seoul   Singapore   Sydney   Toronto

1 2 3 4 5 6 7 8 9 0   FGR/FGR   0 1 0 9

ISBN: 978-0-07-149631-5
MHID: 0-07-149631-9

This publication is designed to provide accurate and authoritative information in regard to the subject matter covered. It is sold with the understanding that neither the author nor the publisher is engaged in rendering legal, accounting, or other professional service. If legal advice or other expert assistance is required, the services of a competent professional person should be sought.

—*From a Declaration of Principles jointly adopted*
by a Committee of the American Bar
Association and a Committee of Publishers

McGraw-Hill books are available at special quantity discounts to use as premiums and sales promotions, or for use in corporate training programs. To contact a representative please visit the Contact Us pages at www.mhprofessional.com.

Library of Congress Cataloging-in-Publication Data
Porrini, Patrizia.
    Above the board : how ethical CEOs create honest corporations / by Patrizia Porrini, Lorene Hiris, and Gina Poncini.
        p. cm.
    ISBN-13: 978-0-07-149631-5
    ISBN-10:   0-07-149631-9
1. Business ethics--United States--Case studies. 2. Chief executive officers--United States--Case studies. 3. Leadership--Moral and ethical aspects--United States--Case studies. 4. Corporate culture--Moral and ethical aspects--United States--Case studies. 5. Moral development--United States--Case studies. I. Hiris, Lorene. II. Poncini, Gina. III. Title. IV. Title: Ethical CEOs create honest corporations.
    HF5387.5.U6P67 2009
    174'.4--dc22
                                                                                2008031905

This book is printed on acid-free paper.

To my mother Vera, my husband, John, and
my little Giovanni Luca.
—Patrizia

To my husband, Hermann, and to our family.
To my friends, colleagues, and students.
—Lorene

In memory of Tarcisio. To my family.
—Gina

Contents

Preface

Is ANYTHING GOOD happening on the ethics front? Is there a definitive approach to encourage a culture of ethics in business, education, and the wider society? Where can we turn for ideas and inspiration? When someone like Eliot Spitzer, who made his name crusading against corporate malfeasance, is embroiled in a scandal that leads to his resignation as Governor of New York, we can only wonder who we can hold above board as an example.

As the twenty-first century began, we witnessed moral meltdowns of epic proportions involving major organizations in both the public and private sectors: WorldCom, Refco, Tyco, Adelphia, Arthur Andersen, Fannie Mae, Enron, AIG. Because of widespread and relentless media attention, the names of ethically compromised firms have become synonymous with unethical behavior, commanding as much recognition as if they were the subject of marketing campaigns. Just think what the name "Enron" conjures up in corporate circles, professional environments, and classrooms.

A 1987 book titled *The Complete Book of Wall Street Ethics* was greeted with loud guffaws and belly laughs. The book consisted of 158 pages: all blank. Times have changed ... or have they? Although a great deal of lip service touting corporate ethics programs was paid in the wake of major corporate scandals, cases of fraud continue to materialize: a rogue trader at a major international bank or the subprime scandal impacting companies too numerous to list. Such breaches of fiduciary responsibility contribute to depicting ethics in business as blank pages in a book.

Though negative examples do not necessarily involve the majority of businesses, ethical deviations continue to be the object of media attention. A multitude of stakeholders are affected by what initially seems like just one minor moral misjudgment or lapse, in one industry, by one group, or even by one person. In fact, ethical deviations may cause a tidal wave and ultimately harm the majority of stakeholders. For example, investors have been shaken by the severe losses that mortgage companies have taken. Mortgage holders are devastated by the immense impact that loose loan screenings are having on their financial standing, with many of them losing the homes they cherish. Consumers are horrified by the sudden metamorphosis in mortgages' terms—from easy to impossible. The social, psychological, or physical costs to victims of ethical misconduct can last for years.

Today, organizations and their leaders come under the constant scrutiny of stakeholders who, in their quest for information, are helped (or overwhelmed) by the proliferation of media reports. Baby boomers, for example, need to build and protect retirement income, and families need to find appropriate mortgage loans and bankers they can trust. Employees now need to direct their own pension planning and are held hostage to the ups and downs of the financial markets. We are all stakeholders, whether as a present or former employee, investor, supplier, manager, pension fund director, regulator, consumer, banker, or even government official. Corporate malfeasance cuts across society and touches us all.

Look at the fraud perpetrated by one young trader, enabled by the failure of oversight. Individuals and businesses have been affected.

Investors' trust in banks and investment houses has been severely compromised and their base capital drastically debased. When confidence in the market mechanism is compromised, corporations' ability to raise funds is extremely impeded. Credit markets seize up, and if corporations cannot raise money to fund other profitable projects, the spillover effect has severe repercussions. Jobs are lost and potential jobs are not created. Costly but necessary supervision and government regulations will follow, to convince the general public that safeguards are in place to prevent a particular lapse from happening again. The cost is ultimately borne by all of us.

We are all ethically vulnerable. Yet it seems the most we can do is try to keep informed, which, at times, can seem like an impossible task.

What's being done to improve the situation? The necessity of regulation such as the Sarbanes-Oxley Act of 2002 in the United States results in costly data gathering and audit fees and procedures, as well as expensive, extensive internal and external controls. And all of this takes management and government away from their respective missions, thereby subtracting from stakeholder returns. If regulations solved the problem and were effective, the time and costs would be justified. However, most often regulations just force compliance. As we've seen, this is not enough to reliably inspire public confidence or encourage a culture of ethics.

Business school accrediting agencies are trying to contribute to a solution, including mandating ethics education in the curriculum as an important component for training future managers. Sincere, successful efforts that preempt malfeasance and immorality and create an environment of honesty and morality are sure to be more effective and long lasting than coerced regulation. However, classroom

cases are often based on theory and tend to focus on the appropriate strategy for adjudicating ethical "gray areas." Although encouraging intense discussion of complex ethical issues, isolated examples
often lead to "gray" solutions that have few direct applications in
the real world. Students can easily identify basic black-and-white ethical issues as right or wrong, but problematic gray-area issues viewed
in isolation often result in compromised outcomes.

What about business leaders? Surely things cannot be as bleak as
the scandals of the moment suggest. Surely there are numerous leaders who feel strongly about cultivating an ethical environment in their
organizations. As professors in business programs, we felt a need for
positive role models to present to our students, especially since more
and more business schools are incorporating courses on ethics into
their curricula. We set out to discover what we could learn from those
CEOs who care deeply about encouraging ethical behavior and who
were willing to share their views, stories, initiatives, and even their
difficult moments at the helm. The result of our investigation into the
key things business is doing today to encourage a culture of ethics is:
Above the Board: How Ethical CEOs Create Honest Organizations.

The purpose of our book is to understand the practices, procedures, and personalized approaches employed by our contributing
CEOs that foster a more ethical business climate. This book offers
concrete examples of ethics in action. It also shows how CEOs tell
stories as a way to keep values alive and how they reap the benefits
of ethical challenges and difficulties. It discusses tangible steps to help
harness ethical energy and to make ethics messages far-reaching. It
examines how companies are ethically alert to the external environment, how leaders address future generations, and how ongoing
efforts are actually making ethics contagious.

ABOVE
THE BOARD

Introduction

Building Honest Organizations

THE SUMMER OF 2003 was a memorable one for the 13,000 former Abbott Laboratories employees who were about to become Hospira, Inc., a prominent global hospital products manufacturer that provides its customers with medication delivery devices and injectable pharmaceuticals. A particular date stands firm in the mind of Christopher B. Begley, Chairman and CEO of Hospira. It was August 23, 2003, when he and his colleagues at the core global hospital products organization of Abbott were informed that they would have the once in a lifetime opportunity to create a totally new, independent company with leading products, devoted employees, a solid revenue stream, and a strong customer base.

In describing this transition, Begley highlighted the importance of Hospira's already solid foundation. "Unlike many other companies—both old and new—we had a solid foundation from which to grow and a unique opportunity to look at our business from a fresh perspective."

Rather than dwell on possible negative aspects of the reorganization, Begley and his staff looked at the potential of the change. Begley notes that shortly after the former Abbott employees began to absorb the news that they would be part of a new organization, they were overcome with excitement at the prospects that lay before them. In the minds of Begley and many of his colleagues, there was a need for a fresh start.

"When we spun off from Abbott," Begley noted, "we inherited some major assets. But we also saw the need for big changes. We had spent 70 years functioning inside a very big corporation, which meant we had decades of predictable, stable performance and secure and proud employees. This also meant we had a long-standing inherited culture. We knew that some of this inheritance would serve us well in the future, and some of it would need to evolve, to serve a new and different company."

Begley saw that there was much work to be done before an independent, publicly traded Hospira could be realized. "To guide us, one of the very first projects we undertook was the invigorating challenge to define our company through a vision, values, and commitment platform," he noted. "This was a project that I, along with the members of my immediate staff, undertook with great pride and enthusiasm. We wanted to develop something that came straight from our hearts and would speak directly to each employee. Something that, in a few words, would capture the attitudes and behaviors we wanted all Hospira employees to embody."

After Begley and his colleagues articulated Hospira's vision—"Advancing Wellness™ through the right people and the right products"—they were able to establish two key company pillars: Hospira's commitment statement and its core values.

Hospira's commitment statement provided the new enterprise with, as Begley observed, "a road map for serving our key stakeholders: customers, employees, shareholders, and communities." The second company pillar—its value statement—was written, said Begley, "to emphasize several key principles that would drive our ability to achieve our vision and deliver on our commitments: integrity, ownership/accountability, speed, and entrepreneurial spirit—the most important of which is integrity." He added, "From the moment we learned of our impending spin-off, I knew that I wanted integrity to be synonymous with our company."

That Hospira chose to make integrity—above so many other competing commitments—its defining platform from its inception has proven extremely valuable to the company's development. Integrity served as a solid foundation for the fledgling enterprise and its employees during the tumultuous times of change following the spin-off. The leadership of Hospira had the foresight to understand that if integrity was emphasized early on in the company's history, it was more likely that its value would be embedded into the company's culture, paving the way for long-term business success.

"We had studied the legacy of respected leaders who emphasized integrity, so we knew that this value was integral to business success. Integrity is even more important in today's business climate, given the added pressure of being successful in the face of the market's focus on short-term results," Begley said. "Assuming that new—and even greater—challenges will face the global marketplace in the future, it can and will be difficult to stay the ethical course."

As to why Hospira puts so much emphasis on integrity, Begley explained: "Because we're convinced that it's fundamental to developing a company where people communicate genuinely and openly, in an atmosphere of trust. We want a company where people aren't driven by fear and where they take responsibility for their actions, yet they function effectively as team members."

Begley thus articulated the benefit of laying integrity down as a strong, unwavering foundation upon which an enterprise is built. It gives employees and stakeholders the framework to act freely within the boundaries and perimeter of the corporate fabric. Word and behavior must be aligned. However, as Begley articulated, "Integrity can't be some vague, airy principle to which people give lip service but don't reflect in their actions or behavior. The word must have real, in-depth meaning."

Begley also draws on stories from the company's past and present, which suggest that Hospira's founding values are alive and deeply rooted. "One of my favorite examples of integrity in action is a story I often tell about a Hospira manager," recalled Begley. "He had completed his annual goals, knowing that the amount of his bonus depended on meeting stated commitments. When he received his bonus, he was surprised. He ran the calculations and said, 'You know, you paid me too much. You need to correct it.' After doing a bit of investigation, we discovered that, sure enough, he was right. We corrected the mistake and offered our sincere thanks to this person. To this day, I hold him in the highest regard."

Begley has his own Hospira launch-related anecdote to help illustrate how integrity and trust can come into play in even the simplest of situations. "When Hospira first went public, I was given the opportunity to ring the opening bell at the New York Stock Exchange," he said. "The woman in charge unveiled an extremely complex control box, and just a few seconds before the opening, she told me simply to 'push the red button.' One problem: I'm color blind, and therefore had no idea what button to press. Of course, I couldn't be responsible for the delayed opening of America's capital markets, so I blurted out, 'I'm color blind!' The woman showed me which button to push, and the opening-bell ceremony went off without a hitch."

Begley feels that this story demonstrates several things, most importantly integrity: "First, I had to acknowledge that I needed help. Second, another person had to step forward to help me. Third, I needed to trust that person. Without integrity, you can't have trust or teamwork."

The anecdotes of the honest manager and the opening bell underscore the importance of stories in giving context to values—and to honesty. Underlying the words "value" and "integrity" is an honest, open, and trusting relationship between employee and employer, between one individual and another.

The responsibility of nurturing integrity in business is, in Begley's view, both a challenge and privilege that future leaders must undertake. He cites a University of Michigan Business School survey on the importance of integrity in today's global economy. The survey found that 84 percent of top executives believe that the study of business ethics is either "very important" or "critical" to being a successful CEO. Only business strategy ranked higher.[1]

Hospira's vision, values and commitment have served as the company's guiding principles from Day One, Begley underlines. "They were designed with the notion that if we do ingrain them in the hearts and minds of our employees, they will give our company the best possible chance for establishing a culture that drives our business strategies and success. Our value of integrity, in particular, remains

---

[1]"Future of Management Education Summary Technical Report," University of Michigan Business School and eePulse, Inc., September 2002.

a guiding force when Hospira colleagues are called on to make tough decisions and address challenging situations. In elaborating about integrity, we say, 'We build respect and trust in our company, products and employees by setting high standards and acting on our values.' "

David W. Bernauer, the former CEO[2] of Walgreen Co., explained how his company spreads a culture of trust: "Repeat, repeat, repeat. We have three things going for us as we strive to spread our culture of trust. First is a strong belief, starting with our board of directors, that it's worth spending time and dollars to make sure the trust upon which we built our past is manifested in all we do in the present and future. This is a message you can't overcommunicate. It must be repeated, repeated, repeated. As Mae West once said, 'Too much of a good thing is wonderful.' "

Bernauer's comments show us that Walgreens understands how to direct its energy toward building ethical awareness. The company is focused on its strong foundation, but also appreciates that its values will help carry the company forth to the future. Walgreens makes clear to its employees that their efforts are not insignificant.

The second thing Walgreens has going for it, Bernauer said, is a "willingness to communicate candidly and credibly to our employees, our customers, and the outside world." Most important, in his view, is employee communication. "If our employees don't understand our culture, how can they treat customers the way we desire?" he asked. "We communicate in all the traditional ways, including the oldest

---

[2]Mr. Bernauer retired as CEO in 2006 and as Chairman in 2007. He was succeeded by Jeffrey A. Rein.

continuously published employee magazine in America. We use our e-mail network and intranet to reach people electronically, especially through a Monday morning message from me to all employees chainwide."

Called the "Dose of Dave," this message sliced through the organizational chart. It allowed Bernauer to talk directly and casually to, as he called them, "our folks, many of whom I'll never have the opportunity to meet. It lets me say thank you . . . or comment on an issue that's put us on the evening news. It lets me explain why we're changing something . . . or why we're not. It lets me say we screwed up when things go haywire."

"Better yet," added Bernauer, "there's a reply button that lets employees bypass bureaucracy and write directly to me. And they do."

Bernauer's actions as CEO show he was clearly committed to maintaining his personalized reach with all employees. He stayed involved. He used different modes of outreach, with the Monday morning Dose of Dave message allowing him to remain casual with employees. His comments and his actions highlight the key role the CEO plays in building a climate of ethics.

"Our third pro-trust advantage? It's by far the most important, because it's impossible to replicate: the long service and experience of Walgreen employees," Bernauer noted. "Consider this: Our company is 107 years old, our median store age is just 6.3 years, and our average years of experience for store managers is 12.6. Long service is respected and valued. The joke here is that at 20 years, you're still a Walgreen 'teenager.' Every two months, our magazine celebrates more than 100 people achieving 25 years or more of service. My 40 years is nothing unusual: In the history of our company, we've had 56 people achieve 50 or more Walgreen years."

The long-service record of the company's employees sends a powerful message to Walgreens' young, new employees. Said Bernauer, "It provides the example of people in a variety of positions who know how to treat customers well, and it says, 'This must be a pretty good place to work.' We could not have achieved our position in American retailing over the past several decades without our solid core of long-service employees."

Bernauer's actions promoted not only loyalty but also each employee's sense of belonging. They were prompted to consider the effects of their judgments on the long-run success of Walgreens. By taking ethics down to the individual level and endeavoring to inform its employees of their importance to the company, Walgreens is able to keep trust alive.

Walgreens is further personalized by the importance it places on the members of the company's founding family. In fact, the company so respects its founders that the Walgreen family name is above the door of each of their drugstores. "This has been the case for 107 years," Bernauer explained. "The family name above the doors is a personal element that stands for trust. From 1901 through 1998, Walgreen had just three Chairmen: Charles R. Walgreen Sr., the founder; his son, Charles R. Walgreen Jr.; and his grandson, Charles R. Walgreen III. The founder's great-grandson, Kevin Walgreen, is a Store Operations Senior Vice President today.

"The family name is not listed as an asset on our balance sheet, but, for my money, it belongs there. And this has nothing to do with financial control," Bernauer continued. "We are a Fortune 50, publicly traded corporation, and the Walgreen family has not owned anything close to a controlling interest since our earliest years. But knowing we are the twenty-first century guardians of the philosophy on which Charles Walgreen Sr. founded this business is a powerful incentive to keep those values intact."

Linking past and present, Bernauer said, "I go back to trust." He related that in the early years, "Mr. Walgreen often said the business grew because he was lucky in the men who came to manage his stores. 'I don't know how many times,' said his wife decades later, 'that Charles came home and remarked, "Well, today I hired another man who is smarter than I am.'" Mr. Walgreen couldn't have done that if he didn't trust people.

"More than a century later, it is still how we are building Walgreens," said Bernauer. "Let's start with me. I don't worry about my direct reports. I trust them to do the right thing by Walgreens and to make good decisions. I trust them to own up to their inevitable mistakes and learn from them. That trust goes down the line to their reports, and on and on."

The Walgreens operating model was designed to provide support to its stores in a way that would best serve their customers. At the same time, the company's culture of trust allows their district managers and store managers to function autonomously, which is very rare among retailers. Along the way, Bernauer noted, a company builds efficiency: "If you trust your employees, you don't waste time worrying about them, and you get a heck of a lot more work done. Most importantly, I've found that when you trust people, they generally live up to your expectations. If they weren't the people smarter than you to start, they become that as their careers progress."

Bernauer reflected on the kinds of influence leaders have. "Any CEO worth his or her salt will tell you that the further they move up in their organization, the less direct influence they have. So, if I cannot trust my colleagues, I am paralyzed as a leader," Bernauer said. "And in trusting them, I am fulfilling . . . my primary responsibilities—to build the leaders who will succeed today's top management team and secure Walgreens' reputation as a good place to work, shop, invest in . . . and to build the leaders who follow, as we do, the earliest mission statement by our founder Charles R. Walgreen Sr.: 'We believe in the goods we merchandise, in ourselves, and in our ability to render satisfaction. We believe that honest goods can be sold to honest people by honest methods.' "

Hospira and Walgreens are just two among an increasing number of companies that recognize that ethics is important to *all* companies, even those that have not been connected to scandals or face "Enron issues." We were fascinated how companies as far ranging as Hospira, Whirlpool, Walgreens, Anadarko, Texas Instruments, Universal Health Services, and others have woven the idea of corporate values and morals into their organization. Even the "average" company—one that doesn't make headlines—recognizes the inherent importance of corporate responsibility. Whether or not the idea of ethical corporations raises eyebrows, there is a huge investment—in terms of money being spent and shareholder value involved—in building a culture of ethics in organizations.

Society is becoming more transparent and business is becoming more transparent. Even the financial services industry, which some people consider the last bastion of less-transparent practices, is evolving into a more accountable business sector. As corporate responsibility has become an emerging issue, we wanted to learn more about what CEOs and their companies are actually doing to encourage an ethical environment in their workplaces.

The ability to build an organization on an ethical foundation is vital in today's complex business world. Being the CEO of a major corporation means giving more attention to your organization's values and principles, especially in light of the changes in the corporate landscape wrought by high-profile scandals.

The ubiquity of negative media reports exposing malfeasant corporations underlines a simple truth with far-ranging implications: Just because something is legal does not mean it is ethical. Though some companies may enjoy a long-standing reputation for integrity, they are not immune to ethical stress. Contributing to a culture of honesty has become a more challenging endeavor, and countless companies are grappling with their duty to be ethically responsible.

The ethical climate of an organization is fundamental in guiding employee behavior, and such a climate depends on leadership and concrete initiatives that encourage continuous adherence to a company's core values. Employees—whether just a few or tens of thousands—are constantly acting on behalf of their company as they go about their day-to-day activities. True, a firm can enact formal codes that stand as a written foundation for employee behavior, but organizations across a range of industries rise to the challenge of fostering an ethical environment that goes beyond compliance. Above all, CEOs are in a position to set the ethical tone and climate of their organizations.

But how, exactly, are CEOs encouraging a culture of ethics and values in their organizations? What are their views? How are they including employees in their initiatives? What are companies actually doing at the urging of their leaders concerned about building an honest organization?

The answers to these questions are not readily apparent: The occasional CEO profile in the media does not provide the wider picture, and the preponderance of reports on scandals and negative incidents presents a biased view of corporate behavior. Our search for positive values showed us the ways many leaders are making innovative and concrete efforts to build honest organizations. We analyzed a wide range of materials from CEOs of Fortune 500 and Standard and Poor's 500 companies. We looked at the stories that get retold time and again in organizations to underscore a company's enduring values. We examined how CEOs build on the founding principles of their organizations. We dissected the way they communicate to their stakeholders about tough times...and how they overcame those tough times. We analyzed their written materials, scrutinized their codes and formal statements, viewed their videos, and pored over their correspondence.

A strong signal is clearly being sent by virtue of the fact that CEOs from a wide range of industries responded enthusiastically to our invitation to put their organizations and their ethics-related initiatives on stage. Ethics is not only good for business, it is vital. One CEO personally responded the same week that we sent him our invitation to participate in our project. Another CEO contributed an array of materials to provide a behind-the-scenes look at his company, including a copy of a speech transcript with his handwritten notes in the margins. Other CEOs sent personalized letters, with their staffs keeping us up-to-date on their written contributions.

As we looked deeper into the materials these executives had provided us, we realized we had a unique opportunity to capture the voices of CEOs who recognized the importance of building values and ethics into their organizations. With a wealth of materials made available to us, we drew on our backgrounds in management, finance, and communications to qualitatively analyze the data.

As we analyzed the materials, we expanded on our original idea to view these positive role models within the wider picture of ethics as an integral and continuously evolving part of business. In their efforts to nurture integrity and trust in their organizations, CEOs build a store of value, with employees across the organization contributing to its ethical capital.

Jeff Fettig, CEO of Whirlpool, is explicit about the importance of ethics: "Having the right strategy is one thing, but having a company with the right values, culture, and capabilities is critical to a successful and sustainable enterprise."

Dave Bernauer, former CEO of Walgreens stated: "People sometimes look at things like trust and ethics and honesty as the soft side of business. They pay it lip service, but they don't connect it with profitability. They're dead wrong. Trust is as good for shareholders as it is for employees and customers. It's not an 'add-on' ... it's the core of business, essential to growth and productivity."

We identified the common denominators of the multiple methods, initiatives, and styles that various CEOs use to encourage a culture of ethics in their organizations. In doing so, they not only ensure compliance but also nurture integrity. Rather than just reporting on problems and solutions or providing a portrait of ethics in business (however fuzzy the concept), we detailed our findings in practical terms, as lessons learned. Additionally, we'll discuss what our study indicates are the best business practices to allow ethics to flourish, using examples based on our analysis of the materials provided by participating CEOs.

Company Values and Stories

Regardless of how old their company is or how long they have been in their positions, the CEOs we surveyed—across the board—relentlessly communicate to their stakeholders that their companies are based upon ethical foundations. One of the main ways these executives do this is through telling stories. As we explore in Chapter 1, years and years of history are not a prerequisite for a CEO's successful implementation of ethics-related initiatives into his or her company. Rather, the CEO needs only to recognize that the company's history and traditions represent valuable building blocks that can make powerful points when they are illustrated through company narratives. We identify the ways CEOs galvanize their relationship with corporate history, as well as how they build on the company's guiding principles to ensure the continued evolution and growth of the organization.

Creating Ethical Buy-In

When CEOs make it possible for each employee to question, share, and develop a set of values that apply to their specific role in the organization, they help create employee buy-in for a culture of ethics. CEOs intent on building honest organizations create opportunities for dialogue among employees. When the employees themselves can contribute to the articulation of their company's values, leaders' efforts to build an ethical climate are more effective. This process fosters employee commitment and allows them to feel as though they have actively contributed to what, on its own, may seem like "just" a well-written statement or code.

Communicating the Challenges of Building an Honest Organization

In Chapter 2, we present insights gleaned from CEOs who have led their organizations through change and other challenges. The CEOs we surveyed were eager to relate the challenges they encountered while building honest organizations, whether their specific difficulty was establishing an ethical identity or facing an industry-specific challenge that threatened their company's reputational capital. We were impressed with the way many CEOs were willing to recall difficult situations to describe how they met the challenges at hand. These CEOs provide inspiration and powerful lessons that contribute to the integrity of their organizations.

Harnessing Ethical Energy

While codes of conduct and ethics statements act as the formal foundations upon which employee compliance is built, their real power is exponentially increased when companies are able to make them come alive for their employees. This is a central point that emerged from our study and it is showcased in Chapter 3. Honest organizations know that it is not enough simply to ensure that the company's codes are visually prominent and carefully articulated. They know that to make employees pay attention to the codes, they must be designed so that they are helpful. Good CEOs also recognize the effectiveness of mixed modes and different channels to spread their company's word.

Creating a Climate of Excitement about Ethics

CEOs act to keep employee enthusiasm and excitement about ethics high, recognizing that written codes and statements alone won't make for an ethical company culture. They do this through an array of means aimed at motivating, recognizing, and inspiring people. In Chapter 3 and 4, the CEOs we surveyed detail how they ensure their employees are listened to, and some were explicit about how they gather input from their employees to make their shared values even stronger.

Keeping Ethics Alive: Values Are Steady, Unwavering and Ingrained

CEOs work constantly to "keep ethics alive." Yes, corporate niceties like videos and plaques play a role, but such exercises must be ongoing. Nurturing the work environment requires relentless efforts. CEOs build a kind of ethical endurance and imbue a sense of timelessness into their ethics campaigns, which helps drive their company's day-to-day activities. CEOs keep ethics at the top of people's minds. Honest organizations create a culture that demands, rewards, and models ethical behavior.

Ethics and the External Environment

In their efforts to foster a climate of ethics, the CEOs in our study are alert to the external environment, making sure that the business organization functions optimally. In Chapter 5, they explain that in an ethically aware culture, every employee must be actively involved in bringing the organization to its full potential. At the same time, they acknowledge that the organization is part of a larger environment to which it is accountable. Specifically, employees must be aware that stakeholders will define their company's success.

Creating Future Generations of Business Leaders

CEOs concerned about ethics must pay attention to future generations of business people, a topic explored in Chapter 6. They address aspiring leaders and urge them to consider business ethics education. Ethical leaders reflect on the business community and the role of business in society. They talk about governance, regulation, the reputation of business, industry challenges, and they form partnerships with communities in order to build a climate of ethics that extends outside of the organization.

Ethics Can Be Contagious

By relentlessly communicating about ethics and taking a range of initiatives, ethical CEOs are actually helping to make ethics contagious in their organizations and beyond. In the final chapter, they emphasize that ethical behavior should not be mandated only from a single company. Rather, they assert that there is an industries-wide need for ethical business practices. With the ethical climate of the business world at issue, corporations, associations, and educational institutions need to work together to encourage a widespread culture of ethics.

Chapter 1

Keeping Company Values Alive through Stories

CEOs CONCERNED ABOUT ethics take action to keep their company's history, traditions, and values alive. The CEOs in our study appreciate the ethical foundation of their companies, whether new or long established. Though most of the companies included in this chapter have long histories, younger firms also direct attention to their founding values. This holds true of these younger companies' CEOs and first employees, so a century-long history is not a prerequisite for successfully implementing ethics-related initiatives. What *is* important is recognizing that a company's traditions are valuable building blocks and that its people, past and present, breathe life into its values.

In the stories we analyzed, CEOs make their role in corporate history more vivid. They communicate their commitment to ethics by building on the company's guiding principles. By telling stories that involve other people, they help ensure that they are retold and become part of an organizational dialogue.

How do stories get started? Some CEOs reflect on what they learned growing up. Others highlight significant points in the lives of the company's founders. The late O.B. Goolsby, former President and CEO of Pilgrim's Pride, would speak of Chairman and founder Bo Pilgrim. Pilgrim grew up during the Great Depression, an experience that—along with his religion—was closely connected to his ethical stance. Dave Bernauer, the former CEO of Walgreen Co., recalled life in a small town and the way trust is built in relationships.

When CEOs tell stories about the company's founders, the founders' families, or their own role in establishing a company, these stories become part of the company's shared narrative. They make a company's integrity, honesty, and trust come alive.

When CEOs recall stories that involve individual employees, they underline the contribution each person can make to uphold the company's commitment to ethics. When Jeff Fettig, CEO of Whirlpool, includes anecdotes while describing the company's "Enduring Values," he makes those values more concrete. Many CEOs use narratives to articulate their own key guidelines and taxonomies to promote ethical behavior. While not intended to be formal codes of conduct, these personalized accounts provide structure for an ethical outlook. Stories become part of organizational memory as they are retold and shared.

CEOs intent on building honest organizations live very much in the present, but they are able to look at the past and identify the threads that connect people, relationships, and values to the organization. We found countless examples of how CEOs use the past to invigorate the present. We'll start with Dave Bernauer, former CEO of Walgreen Co.[1]

---

[1]Mr. Bernauer retired as CEO in 2006 and as Chairman in 2007. He was succeeded by Jeffrey A. Rein.

Building a Culture of Trust

David W. Bernauer, former CEO of Walgreen Co., recalled life in a small town and the way trust is built in relationships. "That same culture of trust is probably the major thing that has kept me at Walgreens for almost 40 years," he said. He grew up in rural Minnesota where his father was the manager of the JCPenney store. "Everyone knows everyone in small towns," he explained. "Relationships are close and people rely on each other. That builds trust, and trust is the core of high ethical standards."

Bernauer was quick to point out that this is not a romantic portrait of life in the 1950s heartland. "It's like that today," he said. He still sees the same values when he's at his family's lake cottage near his hometown. "Several years ago, our daughter's boyfriend was visiting and I remember our laughter when he expressed surprise that a farmer could leave his corn on a stand—unattended for hours with a cash box marked '20 cents per ear'—and lose neither corn nor profits."

Bernauer draws on personal experiences and his long career at Walgreens to underline the importance of a culture of trust. He joined Walgreens as a young pharmacist right out of school when the company was much smaller—about 500 drugstores, versus more than 6,000 today.

"Our founder's son, Charles Walgreen Jr., ran the company back then, and Chuck was *nothing* if not ethical." Bernauer added that even in his 100th year, Charles Walgreen Jr. would proudly recall how he asked his friend, the president of Rotary International, for permission to distribute Rotary's "Four-Way Test" to Walgreen employees in 1955. Said Bernauer, "Chuck said it built on a line in his dad's creed, written in the company's early years: *We believe we can sell honest goods to honest people by honest methods."*[2]

> The principles of the "Four-Way Test" remain the touchstone for Walgreen Co.
>
> Is it the truth?
> Is it fair to all concerned?
> Will it build good will and better friendship?
> Will it be beneficial to all concerned?

Said Chuck Walgreen decades later, "If you use a test like that for the things you say or do, you won't be making mistakes."

According to Bernauer, some people think the Four-Way Test is hokey . . . and that Walgreens is old-fashioned to rely on those words. "You may feel that way yourself. I can only tell you that from my perspective working my way up through the company's ranks, *it works*," he noted, adding, "I'm not saying we never make mistakes, or that we've never dealt with dishonesty or unfair treatment of employees or customers. As a recent Walgreen advertising campaign said: *We don't live in a town called 'Perfect.'* "

Why is a test like this—one that even the CEO realizes may appear "hokey"—effective?

Pride in core values is the first part of the answer: Pride in the organization, pride in people, pride at all levels, and, above all, pride

---

[2]Charles W. Walgreen Jr. died in 2007 shortly before his 101st birthday.

at the top. Bernauer shows pride in an approach that, in his words, might make some people think Walgreens is "old-fashioned." The son of Walgreens' founder showed the pride his father showed. Pride permeates the organization.

Simplicity is another part of the answer. Four straightforward questions—the Four-Way Test—represent core values, which are woven into Walgreens' business practices. In the materials we analyzed, simplicity helps make key points more widely applicable and at the same time memorable.

Telling stories is the final part of the answer. Bernauer tells stories about the Four-Way Test and personalizes values. "That test is alive," he said, and the stories he tells—and others tell—help keep it alive. "It's on plaques in stores and corporate offices. We refer to it frequently in verbal and written communication. One of our vice presidents was working with the head of our legal department on a sensitive lawsuit a few years ago. 'We met about it one morning,' she said, 'and he told me he'd been pondering the case and asking himself, *are we meeting the Four-Way Test?*' " This type of scrutiny is not unusual, according to Bernauer, who repeats Chuck Walgreen's words, "If you use a test like that for the things you say or do, you won't be making mistakes."

Pride in core values, simplicity, and stories help to ensure the effectiveness of the test as an ethical guide for employees. Making these practices a simple yet key part of their "way of business" has helped Walgreens to sustain a culture of high ethical standards as they grew to over 6,000 stores all over the United States.

Honesty, truth, fairness, building better friendships and relationships with customers are values integral to small town life. Whereas many companies might seem to focus on profits only, Walgreens has focused on the best practices to enjoy a long, prosperous history and a top position in the industry. Years later, this culture of trust is part of their corporate personality. It underlies how they approach corporate decisions on a day-to-day basis.

In the cases we analyzed, CEOs keep stories and values alive by various means. CEO Dave Bernauer keeps the test—and core values—alive by showing pride in Walgreens' core values and its people, by telling stories that go back in time, and by quoting members of the founding family. But that is only part of what he does. He was also quick to point out the relevance of the test—and the core values today. He recognizes how the company's core values help in dealing with unusual, unforeseen situations. The Four-Way Test connects people in dispersed locations and builds a culture of trust.

Stories as a Way to Sustain Core Values

What else has contributed to sustaining core values in Walgreens? Bernauer himself recognizes the importance of stories. He quoted U.S. business writer Tom Peters, who said, "Nothing reveals more of what a company really cares about than its stories and legends . . . listening to a company's stories is the surest route to determining its real priorities and who symbolizes them." Bernauer also referred to the Native American Hopi tribe, which expressed the same thoughts in a few simple words: "Those who tell the stories rule the world."

Bernauer is convinced. From Aesop to Shakespeare to Spielberg, good storytellers have hooked us with their tales, he said. "Our Walgreen leaders have worked for decades to do the same thing. We believe that it's not what we say but what we do that ingrains values in our fast-growing employee population," he noted. "So we talk about what we do, not to boast, but to recognize our people who practice ethical behavior in memorable ways."

One of Bernauer's favorite stories is about a store operation vice president who found a three-inch thick notebook marked "Confidential" on an airplane some years ago. Inside were the operating figures, discount information, and virtually every piece of financial data for one of Walgreens' largest competitors. The VP brought it to Bernauer's predecessor, Dan Jorndt. Bernauer said that although Jorndt was sorely tempted, "Dan dropped it in a FedEx envelope addressed to the competitor with a note saying, '*We didn't peek.*' " Two days later, Jorndt received a call from the competitor's chairman saying how glad he was someone from Walgreens had found the book because, "you guys do the right thing."

Stories such as this serve to instruct employees on what it means to be a part of Walgreens. It speaks to the simple question: "How do we exemplify Walgreens' values?"

Bernauer heard that story repeated often. It describes how one can apply personal values to work. Such a story lives far beyond a moment or a specific year. It crystallizes the theme of "doing the right thing" and adds the implicit clause "no matter what." It brings recognition to all of Walgreens' employees—not just the key actor. And it inspires them to build a similar story of their own. Key themes are not only remembered, they are enshrined.

Bernauer knows how important it is to keep stories such as this one alive. Keeping stories alive is difficult in a company of 226,000 employees, where 25,000 jobs are added each year and thousands of new people are hired because of natural turnover. Turnover and a multitude of locations pose a challenge to ethical continuity.

Communication plays a vital role in building a culture of trust. Verbal and nonverbal communication—words and actions—work together to build an ethical organization. Stories use words to describe actions. They are a form of recognition. They crystallize key ethical themes, and as they are repeated over and over, they gain momentum. As much as they promote values, they are a uniting force. They create a sense of ownership and belonging among those connected to the stories. They are a constant amid changing events and become part of organizational memory. This in turn helps inculcate the organization's value system into newcomers and helps socialize them. Stories connect people in the organization to predecessors and foster a sense of continuity.

Dialogue and Enduring Values

In a similar vein, Whirlpool Corporation has steadfastly adhered to its set of "Enduring Values," which focus on "respect, teamwork, diversity, and integrity." Jeff Fettig, Whirlpool President and CEO, said that the company has had a very serious approach to values and ethics for over 100 years.

Whirlpool's set of Enduring Values are a key element of their strategic architecture. "Our Enduring Values are the articulation of the ethics and standards we require" Fettig explained. "They withstand the test of time and are unchanging over strategies, approaches, and competitive eras.

"Whirlpool's Enduring Values were first articulated in 1995," Fettig noted. "Before this, they were the invisible script that guided behavior, but articulating them and calling them out made them visible and turned them into a dialogue, not a laminated wallet card." Indeed, the company benefited from input from thousands of employees in focus groups representing all aspects of Whirlpool.

CEOs intent on maintaining core values and building honest organizations ensure opportunities for dialogue among employees. When the employees themselves can contribute to the articulation of values, efforts to foster an ethical climate are more effective. Employees make sense of their organizational experience as they identify actions that exemplify their values in corporate life. In this example, the CEO ensures that values are articulated, and a constructive hands-on process wins over employees.

Acknowledging the company culture that has driven their actions for a century, Whirlpool employees identified four enduring values: Respect, Teamwork, Diversity, and Integrity. These values remained unchanged for years, until a fifth was added: The Spirit of Winning.

Integrity is the centerpiece of the set of Enduring Values. "We have a deep understanding with our people that *there is no right way to do a wrong thing*," affirmed Fettig.

The second value, *Respect*, centers on respecting each other, respecting the individual, respecting the customers. "This is something that is important to the company," Fettig underlined.

The third value, *Teamwork*, is a cultural belief "about how we want to work with each other," said Fettig.

The fourth value, *Diversity with Inclusion*, creates an inclusive environment where everybody can contribute, where there are no barriers for people to perform, valuing diverse ideas, diverse people, diverse backgrounds, diverse experiences, which leads to better ideas, "and I think a more rewarding workplace," stated Fettig.

The fifth value, *Spirit of Winning*, "starts with the belief and internal drive that being status quo or better than last year is not good enough," Fettig noted. "Whirlpool's culture and values enable individuals and teams to appropriately reach and take pride in extraordinary results and further inspire the 'spirit of winning' in all of us."

A story that exemplifies integrity is still retold within the company—almost a century after it took place. In 1911, when 100 motor-driven wringer washers were delivered to a new customer and a component failed, Whirlpool cofounder Lou Upton replaced the defective part, even though he was not required to do so. As a result, the client doubled the order to 200 washers.

This anecdote underscores Whirlpool's philosophy of integrity in everything it does. It also exemplifies the level of responsibility that Whirlpool feels toward each customer. Whirlpool's relationship with its customers extends beyond the point of sale. The promise to serve customers is embodied in Whirlpool's mission, which encompasses all employees: "Everyone . . . Passionately Creating Loyal Customers for Life." The story about serving a customer in 1911 reminds people of the company's solid foundation.

The text showing how Whirlpool articulates Integrity (see below) depicts what the value means, but it is broader than just words. "The values are an agreement between Whirlpool and each employee," Fettig said. "They describe the expectations and aspirations that we hold for each of us and for the enterprise."

Integrity

We conduct all aspects of our business in an honorable way, recognizing there is no right way to do a wrong thing.

You can expect Whirlpool to:

- Create and communicate high standards of conduct.
- Engage in business activities that are consistent with its reputation for integrity and quality.
- Provide you with support in making ethical and legal decisions.
- Refuse to tolerate unethical, illegal, or unprofessional conduct.
- Emphasize the importance of protecting the confidentiality of all business and employee information.

Whirlpool expects you to:

- Act with personal and professional integrity with fellow employees and with partners and suppliers.
- Understand and comply fully with the letter and the spirit of all laws, regulations, rules, and practices.
- Consult openly with your supervisor, or appropriate others, whenever in doubt about any decision or action being the right thing.
- Safeguard the confidentiality of information about the company and fellow employees.

Values may be open to interpretation. As Fettig put it, "Values can be interpreted somewhat differently by different people." In the case of Whirlpool, he noted, "Holding workshops or open dialogue meetings in work teams to discuss these values has been instrumental in shaping behavior, gaining alignment, and working through the dilemmas that arise as we apply the values to our decisions.

"These values embody the kind of company we are and the kind of company that we want to become. To bring these values to the forefront and embed them in our people," continued Fettig, "we hold numerous dialogues and workshops where we discuss integrity and the dilemmas of everyday work that challenge our behaviors." Creating opportunities for employees to share thoughts, synchronize views, and harmonize their conclusions is a key practice. Through such dialogues, values take root.

We can see that Whirlpool's workshops and open dialogue meetings are instrumental for the company to uphold and adhere to its Enduring Values. These events are opportunities for employees to recognize one common definition and consider the application of these enduring values.

"With dialogue, stories, and ongoing emphasis, integrity is the centerpiece of our values," Fettig noted. "Integrity is not a set of words, it is not a program, and it is not a short-term set of actions for an immediate benefit. Integrity is a part of the fabric of our company that goes back to the very origins of our company and is taught, embedded, and expected in every person at Whirlpool to guide the thoughts, actions, and decisions of 70,000 Whirlpool people. Ethics and integrity is the way we do business."

In the cases we examined, instructive stories and ethical grounding shape how a company acts. The personal involvement of CEOs is central. Leaders and their companies can make words come alive. Verbalizing these values aids each individual's understanding. When individuals' actions are imbued with greater meaning, both the individuals and their actions become an organizational asset. The process of ethical sense-making lets an individual understand the meaning of a simple word such as "integrity" or "respect" and how it applies to their workplace and their role in it. This is an instrumental part of Whirlpool's success in spreading their "Enduring Values" and making sure the values endure—even with newly hired employees, turnover, and other changes that are a part of organizational life.

Breathing New Life into Solid Principles

Sometimes the challenge involves a reinterpretation of organizational reality, not a new organizational identity—though that might seem a logical step when change takes place. When Richard A. Goldstein joined International Flavors & Fragrances (IFF) as Chairman and CEO in 2000,[3] some of his colleagues felt that the company's reason for being and guidelines for behavior needed to be clarified for IFF's employees. Goldstein, however, recognized the importance of reviewing the past to build an honest corporation, so he began by reviewing a document called "The Pursuit of Excellence," which elucidated the vision and values established by IFF'S founding chairman.

"Once I found 'The Pursuit of Excellence,'" remembered Goldstein, "I realized that we had everything we needed. My job was not to create a new vision or mission, but rather to breathe new life into the principles that had made us the industry leader. Our founder's mission encompassed primacy in taste and smell (our industry), joined with values-driven growth grounded in knowledge, integrity, creativity, and innovation. It also considered the common interests of our fellow coworkers, giving our customers value for money and superb service. This was just as relevant and appropriate in 2000 as when it was developed some 20 years earlier."

---

[3]Mr. Goldstein retired in 2006.

It was essential for Goldstein to build on IFF's solid foundation. He recognized that IFF's vision and values were timeless, but what needed to change was the connection of IFF employees to the mission. Existing interpretations needed to be reinvigorated. Employees needed a new sense of connection.

The foundation was there, Goldstein recognized, making him luckier than many of his counterparts in other businesses. What was lacking was the buy-in that only comes with hands-on involvement and a level of detail that helps to answer such questions as "What does driving 'creativity and innovation' in my part of the business really mean?"

Involvement and dialogue are at the core of inviting buy-in. Goldstein outlined IFF's approach: "We have been addressing these issues at all levels and in all locations across the company. We have conducted meetings with senior executives and regional management, as well as sessions with representative groups of employees that look at both the current and desired states of our corporate culture. It is an iterative process, but one that ultimately provides a very clear behavioral road map for the entire organization."

Goldstein made a key decision to respect and work within the existing customs of the organization for which he was now responsible. This approach contrasted sharply with the typical behavior of the newly empowered leader who institutes new practices as a part of their new regime.

Companies have cultures, personalities, cycles, and patterns of doing things. Goldstein made a specific choice to capitalize on the existing cultural mindset and organizational rhythm. He also chose to re-invite every member to become actively involved. In this case, as Goldstein himself confessed, he was "lucky" that the foundation was there and of good value. However, he addressed a key management issue: how to promulgate the values expressed in the "Pursuit of Excellence" document.

Goldstein's approach of workshops and meetings to help employees visualize the potential of their corporate culture shows that such dialogue is essential. It helps people define and accept their values and discover how values apply to their day-to-day activities. Employees find meaning and connect their practices to the greater organizational mission.

Past Experience and Personalized Guidelines

Goldstein asked a simple question: "Is it difficult to be an ethical company in today's hyper-competitive global marketplace?" He answered himself: "Absolutely not." He outlined the key elements for an ethical company.

Throughout his career—and as head of International Flavors & Fragrances Inc.—Richard A. Goldstein has found three elements to be essential: Leadership, Values, and Systems.

1. **Leadership.** They say that "the fish rots from the head." That may be. But the same point can be made in a positive light. In addition to setting an example for the entire organization, a CEO should appoint a senior leadership team that holds itself to the highest moral and ethical standards.

2. **Values.** A company can have as many anonymous whistleblower hotlines as it wants, but those tools will be worth nothing if it does not also have—and truly live by—a set of corporate values that demands and rewards integrity, honesty, and courage. You must create a culture and an environment in which ethical behavior can not only survive, but also thrive.

3. **Systems.** Once the stage is set with strong leadership and a healthy culture, you must provide the information and tools that explain what kind of behavior is expected and what to do if there are breaches of good conduct. In a multinational company, it is important to provide multiple communication approaches to allow for cultural sensitivities and preferences.

"I spent time early in my career in the public—and private—sectors in Washington, D.C.," said Goldstein. "I was there during the Watergate era, which gave me an 'up close and personal' look at leadership behavior that was not highly ethical, to put it mildly. The experience stayed with me, as did the deceptively simple advice given to me by a business colleague—who just happened to be my boss—a few years later. He said: 'Just do the right thing.' "

Simplicity is key. But doing the "right thing" is not always obvious, especially when the issues one is dealing with are neither black nor white. That is where sound judgment and good character come into play—attributes that are difficult to teach. Goldstein, like other CEOs concerned about building honest organizations, recognized the importance of simple questions to guide behavior. "When my colleagues are facing the difficult gray areas that inevitably confront each of us in our professional and personal lives," he said, "I tell them to ask the following questions."

- Is what I am doing right or wrong? Are my actions a matter of short-term expediency and gain for myself and a chosen few? Might they result in long-term harm to others?
- Can I look at myself in the mirror after doing this? Can I face my family, friends and colleagues?
- Does this decision pass the "sniff test?" If it doesn't smell right, that's a good indication that it's something you shouldn't be doing.

In building honest organizations, CEOs must keep in touch with different points of view and not become isolated. Goldstein recounted a conversation with a fellow CEO: "A friend of mine, when he became head of a global, multi-industry company, said, 'It's amazing how good my ideas have become since I became Chairman.'" Goldstein said that too often, "CEOs get caught up in the glory of making it to the top. They surround themselves with 'yes men' and 'yes women' ... and refuse to hear dissenting points of view. It is important to avoid falling into that trap. We *all* have egos. We *all* want our opinions heard. But all of us—even CEOs—have a lot to learn from others. Let your colleagues help you ... and never let yourself become isolated."

Being open to differing viewpoints is important. IFF'S leadership team, for example, is a diverse group of men and women from various countries around the world. Goldstein welcomes their different backgrounds, skills, working styles, and interests. "But the common thread uniting them—in addition to their commitment to driving profitable growth—is their moral character and ethical behavior," he said. "This is a 'nonnegotiable' with me, and while I accept and encourage prudent risk-taking and even the occasional mistakes that can result, I am completely intolerant of breaches in ethical conduct among my direct reports."

The third element identified by Goldstein, systems, represents some of the tangible measures companies have taken in encouraging a culture of ethics and will be discussed in Chapter 3. These systems are inseparable from such intangibles as shared understanding and buy-in for values.

Core Values that Serve as a North Star

In building honest organizations, CEOs address not only internal but also external audiences. The CEOs themselves may be part of ethics-related initiatives and can emphasize the value of their "ethical capital" built up over time.

For example, Anne Mulcahy, chairman and CEO of Xerox Corporation, does this in the speech she sent us. In delivering remarks at Bentley College's Center for Business Ethics,[4] she explained why Xerox believes that a commitment to social responsibility saved the

---

[4]April 12, 2005.

corporation during the worst crisis in its history. Like other CEOs intent on building an honest company, she considered the past to help describe today:

> I'll start with a brief description of what we're doing today. Social responsibility and business ethics are so engrained in the Xerox culture that it's hard to know where to begin. During the decade of the sixties when Xerox came to prominence in Rochester, New York, and was growing rapidly, the community—like so many others across the nation—was torn apart by race riots and the struggle for social justice. Social responsibility was in its infancy. Centers like yours didn't exist. There were no books to tell CEOs how to behave or what to do.

One of the ways CEOs, including Mulcahy, personalize a company and its history is through stories about its founders and their leadership qualities:

> Fortunately, Joe Wilson—the man who founded Xerox—didn't need a book. He knew instinctively that a healthy Rochester was good for Xerox . . . that a corporation has a moral obligation to give back . . . that no company can operate independent of the community in which its people live and work . . . and that behaving in an ethical and responsible way was not only the right thing to do, it was also good business. He articulated a set of core values. Their enduring relevance is unmistakable and they continue to serve as our North Star.
>
> Through Wilson's leadership, Xerox embraced the problems of the mid-sixties. We donated human and financial resources to the community. We helped start organizations to spur economic growth in

the inner city. We provided hundreds of job opportunities and training. And we launched a diversity program within Xerox that is still recognized as one of the best.

Mulcahy continued to underline the influence of the founder, saying, "Joe's involvement in the civil rights struggles of the mid-sixties forever changed the face of Xerox and set us on a course of social involvement that has become part and parcel of the way we have done business ever since." She explained how the social involvement that Joe Wilson started manifests itself today in a "five-pronged approach," which will be discussed in Chapter 3.

CEOs understand that part of moving forward is having a strong understanding of their organization's past and its roots. They understand that there are strong advantages in building on existing foundations. Similarly, leaders of newer companies lay a strong foundation to build a store of values.

The enduring focus on values brings together the objectives of these CEOs. This was evident in our examination of the materials. The CEOs communicate unwavering values, which contributes to stability. The values of the organizations discussed are not trend-based, or continually changing, or in response to situations. Rather, they are enduring, long-lasting, ingrained, and reinforced at every opportunity. CEOs work to bring new meaning to be mutually constructed by employees, yet rooted in the original pillars that define the organization. The CEO is quick to note and communicate the relevance of a specific scenario to core values—whether it's an employee facing a temptation, employees acting in times of crisis, or other such situations. CEOs tell stories that live beyond moments, scenarios, and decisions. People remember stories. The stories endure.

Protecting a Long-Standing Reputation for Integrity

CEOs concerned about building an honest organization make sure they take advantage of opportunities to underline the role of ethics in the company's foundation. We corresponded with O.B. Goolsby, who was President and CEO of Pilgrim's Pride Corporation up until this book was in its final stages.[5] "Since our company's humble beginnings," Goolsby wrote, "ethics has always played a vital role in how we conduct business with our customers, suppliers, family farmers, and our ever-growing family of Partners."[6] He continued, "Our tremendous industry success is due largely to our incredibly talented workforce and our commitment to do what is right and just in all of our dealings." From the start, Pilgrim's Pride viewed its ethical responsibility as spanning far beyond its physical borders to include all stakeholders.

Today, Pilgrim's Pride is the largest poultry company in the United States and the second-largest in Mexico. A Fortune 500 company with $7.6 billion in net sales for 2007, the corporation employs 55,000 people[7] and processes approximately 45 million birds per week for a total of nearly 9 billion pounds of chicken per year. As Goolsby put it, "that's more than enough chicken to provide a half-pound serving for every man, woman, and child in the world."

The success of Pilgrim's Pride is not a coincidence. It is rooted in great beginnings. Goolsby underlined the ethical foundation of the company, saying, "Although the word 'ethics' wasn't talked about

---

[5]Mr. Goolsby passed away unexpectedly on December 17, 2007.
[6]The company refers to its employees as "Partners."
[7]Source: http://www.pilgrimspride.com/aboutus/.

much in the 1940s, ethics was the basis of our company's foundation and continues to drive everything we do today."

The company's ethical foundation is apparent in its history. "With big dreams, $1,000 in cash, and a $2,500 loan, Aubrey Pilgrim opened a small feed store in the rural town of Pittsburg, Texas," said Goolsby. "Later, Aubrey's brother, Lonnie 'Bo' Pilgrim (who today is Senior Chairman of Pilgrim's Pride Corporation), joined him as a partner in the store."

Early on, the two brothers had been giving away 100 baby chicks with each feed sack purchase, said Goolsby. Farmers would raise the chicks, keep some chickens and bring the rest back to the feed store. "We started selling baby chicks to farmers who brought the chickens back to us to sell," explained Bo Pilgrim in his 2005 autobiography, *One Pilgrim's Progress: How to Build a World-Class Company, and Who to Credit.*[8] As the demand for these chickens grew, the first steps were taken toward creating the modern, vertically integrated chicken company known as Pilgrim's Pride Corporation. Pilgrim's Pride built a key exchange relationship with their most important customers: farmers.

Goolsby underlined the importance of the chairman's vision and the challenge of keeping it alive as a company expands. "Throughout the years of rapid growth and great success," he noted, "we have not lost sight of the ethical principles that continue to guide our company. This all stems from the clear vision of our Chairman, Bo Pilgrim, and his unyielding faith in God."

---

[8]Lonnie "Bo" Pilgrim, *One Pilgrim's Progress: How to Build a World-Class Company, and Who to Credit*, Nashville, Tenn.: Thomas Nelson, Inc., 2005.

Chairman and cofounder Bo Pilgrim grew up during the Depression in the 1930s in the little town of Pine, Texas. In *One Pilgrim's Progress*,[9] he recalled a turning point that shaped his life forever:

> The first day that I left home to live with my grandmother, I walked out in the front yard to a little knoll that had no grass on it. I sat down in the dirt there. It was getting late in the day, and as I looked to the west, the sun was starting to go down. It felt like a moment of a new beginning for me—certainly it was a moment of great change. I began to pray, and as I talked to Jesus, I told Him that if I ever amounted to anything, I would always give Him credit. I'm still obligated to that. I have spent my youth and adult life doing my best to give Him the credit for anything I have accomplished. I'm now seventy-seven years old, and that commitment to the Lord is still a part of my desire—not to be a celebrity for myself but to be a celebrity for Him. It was a decision that changed my life and continues to shape my life.

Bo Pilgrim's character, values, and ethics were profoundly shaped by his early childhood experiences. These deeply instilled beliefs became the foundation for the company that bears his name. Pilgrim built guiding principles into Pilgrim's Pride and understands what a driving force a personal obligation can be. Pilgrim demonstrated how important it is to not waver where a corporation's values are concerned. In spite of the many changes Pilgrim's Pride underwent, its values never changed.

Attention to ethics is vital to a company's continued success. Goolsby shared his thoughts with us, stating that for any public company, "the bottom line—making a profit—is paramount." He continued,

---

[9]Pilgrim, p. 14.

"We are responsible for earning a profit in order to create value for our shareholders. But there's much more to it than that. Ethics plays a key role in our continued survival and success. As we state in our *Partner* handbook, 'Ethics involves the point of view that suggests we live in a glass bowl, and we should feel comfortable with any actions we take, as if they were shared publicly.' We realize that in order to gain and keep the public's trust, we must be honest, transparent, and ethical in all of our business dealings." He concluded, "We keep our word, we follow our Guiding Principle, and we remain true to our values, because it's the right way—and the only way—to do business."

The metaphor of a glass bowl is quite powerful. Ethics is transparency, simply put. It is crucial to make ethical foundations come alive for employees who came before, are still here, and are yet to come.

Business Imperatives: Doing Business the Right Way

William (Bill) Nuti, Chairman and CEO of NCR Corporation, was also quick to recall his company's beginnings: "Ethics and operating with integrity have been long-standing business imperatives at NCR. In fact, it dates back to the very beginnings of the company. Some would say that was the very reason the company known as 'National Cash Register' was founded." Nuti recounted some of the company's history and its foundation based on trust:

> The cash register—or "Ritty's Incorruptible Cashier" as it was dubbed at its inception after its inventor, James Ritty—essentially

curtailed inaccuracy and dishonesty. Prior to its invention, retailers and tradesmen employed various and disorganized methods of keeping accounts, resulting in a great deal of confusion and lost profits, not to say numerous opportunities for pilferage or piquing clerks' temptations.

The cash register was the business innovation upon which John H. Patterson founded NCR, Nuti said. "Patterson saw the cash register's potential to record and store transaction information so that both the retailer and customer were assured of an accurate accounting in the trade of goods and services," he said. "While that practice is now a basic tenet of everyday business, it was truly a revolutionary concept in 1884."

According to Nuti, Patterson's genius was his ability to create the demand for a receipt rather than just trying to sell the cash register. Thanks in large part to Patterson's promoting its value, the receipt has become universally accepted as the permanent record of a transaction and is today one of the most powerful pieces of paper. A 1912 company brochure stated: "A receipt, like a deed, is proof of title to property."

Patterson is also recognized as one of the pioneers of modern salesmanship, Nuti explained: "Sales was a vocation that wasn't necessarily held in the highest regard in the late 1800s, Nuti pointed out. "Prior to Patterson's efforts, salesmen weren't often thought of as more than cigar-puffing, whiskey-drinking, wheelers and dealers who would do anything to make a sale, whether employing ethical means or not."

The key to success, Patterson was convinced, was through sales agents, "but not if they appeared slovenly or behaved in an unethical manner," said Nuti. Patterson immediately went to work, molding his sales personnel into better representatives of the company by holding them to the highest standards.

"Recognizing that a company is no better than the behavior that is encouraged not just within its four walls but as it relates to its dealings with customers and partners," explained Nuti, "Patterson believed that a company had to earn the trust of its customers as well as its employees. This attention to doing business the right way permeates NCR's culture."

In this example, we can see the importance of trust as part of NCR's foundation. Once again, the significance of enduring values and timelessness comes to the fore.

Articulating a Philosophy and Making it Available to All Concerned Parties

Michael Coppola, president and CEO of Advance Auto Parts, told us that his company draws on foundations established by its founder, Arthur Taubman, which are today articulated in its "Four-Point Philosophy."

Now completing its seventy-fifth year of operation, Advance Auto Parts remains committed to the Four-Point Philosophy established back in 1932 by Taubman. Advance communicates these tenets to each newly hired employee, and continually through the company's *Team Member Handbook*. This philosophy states that a good company must:

1. Provide a value to its customers by offering quality products at affordable prices
2. Have a solid reputation, because nothing replaces honesty and integrity
3. Keep its goal in mind at all times, by pleasing every customer with service and items that make him or her want to return
4. Treat Team Members with love and respect—like a family

Advance Auto Parts uses not only a team metaphor but also a family metaphor. Advance Auto Parts' *Team Member Handbook* outlines its "Code of Ethics & Business Conduct," by which Advance expects every team member and vendor to abide. In Chapter 4, we focus on initiatives taken by companies to ensure ethical behavior, and we include Coppola's detailed description of the elements of the code.

Making Character a Top Priority: Safeguarding Reputational Capital

Reputations are built over time. A foundation based on high standards, or timeless values, is one element of a good reputation we've discussed. Another concerns key practices such as attracting and hiring the right people.

"I believe that reputation is one of the most important assets for any business, and should be guarded carefully," said Alan B. Miller,

Chairman, President, and CEO of Universal Health Services (UHS). As founder of UHS, Miller is sensitive to the need to safeguard reputational capital and the importance of time in building a reputation. "While it takes a lifetime to develop a good one, it can vanish overnight," he said. "And once a company's reputation has been tarnished, it becomes very difficult to regain it. I have believed this my entire life, and it has infused everything I've done in business."

Employing the right people is paramount. Companies evolve successfully using founding practices as traditions—and some traditions may evolve. They are refined and reframed later, but most help build a sense of responsibility that is taken on by newcomers to protect the business founded and nurtured by their predecessors. Miller's comments underline this key point. "When I founded Universal Health Services over a quarter century ago, I surrounded myself with honest and ethical people—colleagues who shared the same values that I have," he explained. "I wanted these values to pervade our workforce and it's been a guiding principle of the company ever since. While I can't personally know every employee today—we have 35,000—like I did 25 years ago, I have continued to make character a top priority. I suspect that this will remain the case when I'm gone."

Thousands of employees act and make decisions on behalf of their employers every day. Gray areas are ever-encroaching, making ethics important for all companies and making ethical leadership even more challenging. When character is made a top priority, as in Miller's case, the benefits are carried over when employees grow into the thousands. In these examples, we can see how behavior and words allow core values to endure. They are bolstered by stories that put those values into action.

A foundation of strong values means that in times of need, a store of ethical capital can serve as a protective cushion. In the next chapter we consider how CEOs have led their organizations through change and how they deal with challenges. In recounting what happened and how they reached decisions, these CEOs provide inspiration and powerful lessons.

Chapter 2

Reaping the Benefits of Challenges and Difficulties

CEOs INTENT ON building honest organizations share their experiences in dealing with challenging situations. Sometimes this means coming to terms with a major change and other times it means coping with difficulties that come to a head. Even companies with a long tradition of ethical behavior may find themselves facing times of ethical stress.

We were impressed at how many CEOs were candid about problems and challenges. We were intrigued by their accounts of how they led their organizations through change. They have used their abilities in diverse ways, whether establishing an ethical identity for the organization, restoring ethical capital to get back on track, or facing an industry-specific challenge threatening the company's reputational capital. They have carried forth lessons learned from previous experiences and have dealt with the necessity of self- and external regulation.

Not all challenges are necessarily negative. By their very nature, however, they involve difficulties. In the case of Hospira, presented in the Introduction, Chairman and CEO Christopher B. Begley seized the chance to create a culture of integrity unique to the company. In this case, the challenge was positive, and it occurred at the company's formation.

But even when this is not the case, we found that rather than hide a difficulty, the CEOs in our study use it to galvanize people and build trust.

We have chosen specific cases because we feel they embody the different kinds of challenges CEOs and their companies face. There is much to learn from the fortitude of these leaders. We can also learn from the different ways they communicate about their challenges.

Sometimes it is the business or organization itself that poses a challenge. Walgreens, for example, is unlike many companies whose employees report to work in one or just a few key locations, allowing them closer ties to the CEO and corporate culture. Walgreens' thousands of stores are geographically dispersed. Its managers are responsible for carrying out its legendary creed, along with the ethical practices it entails. Dispersion may pose a challenge to maintaining a culture of ethics, but Walgreens demonstrates seamless ethical cohesion.

Building a culture of trust encourages ethical behavior and adherence to the company's core values. A culture of trust, for example, makes it more likely that employees know how to act on their own in an unexpected event. This was borne out when Walgreen Co. faced what former CEO Dave Bernauer called "the greatest operational challenge in our history"—Hurricanes Katrina, Rita, and Wilma in 2005.

Katrina, which caused 75 stores to close and cut off communication to thousands of Walgreens employees, was particularly difficult. Bernauer said that the Four-Way Test wasn't referred to directly as he and his team met in their "disaster room" at 7 a.m. each morning, but it underpinned every decision they made. They provided immediate jobs and financial relief to any Katrina-affected Walgreens employee anywhere in the country, filled $9 million worth of emergency prescriptions free of charge for displaced patients, and sent a convoy of 50 recreational vehicles to house homeless employees, as well as many of the several hundred pharmacists, technicians, and store managers who volunteered to help reopen Walgreens' pharmacies.

Bernauer expressed pride at the way the Four-Way Test guided people's behavior. "It was an amazing effort and I am immensely proud of people throughout the company. We didn't do it for the publicity … we did because it was 'fair and beneficial to all concerned.'"

Weathering the Storm … and Reaching Top Rankings as an Ethical Corporation

Anne M. Mulcahy, Chairman and CEO of Xerox Corporation, described the nucleus of their business ethics program as "part and parcel of our management process, our culture, our DNA," in Chapter 1. Xerox was ranked number one in its industry in *Fortune*'s 2005 "Global Most Admired Companies" list. And *Business Ethics* magazine ranked Xerox number ten among all American corporations in terms of business ethics in 2005. Yet Xerox, too, experienced a time when, in Mulcahy's words, "things unraveled."

In speaking at Bentley College's Center for Business Ethics,[1] Mulcahy candidly recalled a difficult time. Her words provide an

---

[1]April 12, 2005.

opportunity to learn not only about how difficulties came to a head and how the CEO dealt with them, but also to gain insight into how a CEO communicates about difficulties and how she deals with them. Although actions are said to speak louder than words, words can rally people to action and keep their spirits alive. Communication and, especially, dialogue are key to gaining commitment in even the best of circumstances, and they become all the more important when facing exceptional events.

Effective CEOs are willing to communicate about problems. Indeed, Mulcahy began her narrative with disarming frankness, underlining rather than hiding negativity. She personalized her account by means of the first person "I," yet she was also quick to use the plurals "we" and "our," underlining the collective nature of the positive situation just a year earlier, soon to be followed by a series of less positive events.

> Come back with me for a minute to a point in Xerox history I don't ever want to visit again—May of 2000. Just a year earlier, things at Xerox appeared to be extremely positive. Our market share was improving. Competition was faltering. Our financials were sound. The growth in our stock was outpacing the market by a fair amount. A change in leadership had apparently gone well. We were setting our sights on a bright future.
>
> Or so we thought. With alarming speed, things unraveled in the latter part of 1999 and early 2000. We attempted too much change too fast. Competition stiffened while economies here at home and around the world weakened. We uncovered accounting improprieties in Mexico that led to an S.E.C. investigation and sucked up precious management time. And we took some actions that in the broad daylight of hindsight were dumb.

All these and other forces hit us simultaneously in what we came to call 'The Perfect Storm.'

Mulcahy listed highly positive events—soon to be followed not by one, but by many pressing issues. The troubles were given a name: *perfect*. For Xerox, the use of an adjective normally used in positive contexts highlights an intriguing challenge. It also suggests there was a cumulative rather than one-off event facing management.

We observed that when CEOs shared their experiences, names were often given to even negative things—an event, a point in the past, or in the case of Xerox, the culmination of difficulties. A name makes something identifiable and more "concrete." It is easier to deal with concrete entities as opposed to abstractions. A name also makes a problem easier to consign to the past once it is resolved. The name becomes part of a shared culture. The CEO does not shy away from accepting past difficulties: names identified with difficulties can be cited as learning experiences.

It is therefore understandable when Mulcahy said, "We probably could have managed our way through a few of these issues. But the cumulative impact overwhelmed us, and set us back on our heels." She identifies the myriad ways that Xerox's roots were being shaken:

By May of 2000, we were in deep trouble. Revenue and profits were declining. Cash on hand was shrinking. Debt was mounting. Customers were irate. Employees were defecting. Shareholders saw the value of their stock cut in half and continuing to head south.

That was the day I was named President and Chief Operating Officer and typically the point in a talk like this when I would say that it fulfilled a life-long dream. In truth, it did not. And I accepted the responsibility with equal parts of pride and dread.

Mulcahy took on her leadership position at the moment when the troubles behind the "Perfect Storm" were worsening. In her speech, she identified what could help her lead the organization out of trouble. Viewing these factors in the context of our investigation, we note the different elements that work together to nurture an ethical culture. The rewards for the company are apparent, creating a climate of loyalty and commitment among the customers and the employees.

Mulcahy reflected, "Fortunately, I had not one but two aces in the hole. The first was a loyal customer base that wanted Xerox to survive. And the second was an incredibly talented and committed workforce who love Xerox and would do anything to help save the company."

She told the audience what exactly the organization—"we"—did:

> And so we went to work. We laid out a bold and ambitious plan that had three major planks: focus on cash generation to improve liquidity … take $1 billion out of the cost base to improve competitiveness … and strengthen our core businesses to ensure growth in the future. The results have been stunning in both their magnitude and their swiftness. We've dramatically reduced our debt, improved our cash situation, and returned to profitability. In 2000, Xerox lost several hundreds of millions of dollars. In 2005, we made $859 million.

These results show that loyalty and commitment served Xerox well, as did the ambitious plan laid out by Mulcahy and her team. She was very careful to share this accomplishment with her colleagues, never once taking full credit. In outlining progress, Mulcahy again personalized her comments, letting her voice as

CEO add credibility to the account. Her words remind us of the importance of communicating pride:

> As proud as I am of the financial turnaround, what gives me the greatest satisfaction is the progress we made on the third leg of our strategy—strengthening our core business to ensure future growth. Even as we dramatically reduced our cost base, we maintained research and development spending in our core businesses. In fact, we didn't take a single dollar out of R&D in our core business—not one.
>
> As a result, the last few years have been our biggest new product years in our history. I'm on very firm footing when I tell you that we have the broadest, deepest, best set of offerings in our industry. Our customers are responding. Our equipment sales—a bellwether metric for us—have been up. So we're on our way.

The crisis underway at Xerox did not erode its employees' momentum. Employees need unity in times of crisis. Mulcahy offered a valuable glimpse of what she herself learned in leading the turnaround.

"I'm thrilled to have had the opportunity to lead Xerox through this turnaround," Mulcahy said. "It's been the experience of a lifetime. And in what may be the understatement of all time, I've learned a lot along the way about leadership and trust."

Mulcahy witnessed firsthand the importance of vision: "At the depth of our crisis, all Xerox people really wanted to know is how we would get back on track and that our values would be protected in the process." Learning does not happen immediately, she told the audience:

> So even while Rome was burning, people wanted to know what the city of the future would look like. I plead guilty that I didn't immediately get

the importance of giving people—particularly employees—a clear picture of where we were heading. I believe it was the single most often asked question—not whether or not we would survive, but what we would look like after we came through the crisis. I attribute that to the steely optimism of Xerox people even in the face of extreme adversity. And I took it as a very good sign.

Mulcahy was candid about the needs that employees communicated to her: They needed a vision. A vision allows employees to recognize that they are nearing an ultimate goal—a benchmark, a measure, an objective end. Visions are a uniting force and a motivation to act. Mulcahy recognized the importance of vision and employees' needs for a vision to guide their path through the turmoil. But rather than an exercise in literally crafting a vision statement, Xerox took a different approach. It produced a fictitious business article—with a future dateline—that helped articulate its goals and visions for weathering the crisis.

Mulcahy acknowledged the importance of vision to guide employees through the turmoil, even specifying that the company took a different approach:

> But I must tell you that I'm not very patient with things like vision statements that are exercises in grandiose thinking and not rooted in reality. So we tried something a little different—not a vision statement per se but a fictitious *Wall Street Journal* article written in 2005 about where Xerox was and how we had gotten there. It forced us to express our vision in simple English: to put numbers on paper for revenue, profit, the stock price; to make up quotes of how we would like to be seen by various constituencies; to assure people that our values would emerge intact.

Gaining buy-in and ensuring dialogue are vital. For Xerox, "the vision exercise" allows people to work together to define what the organization should look like in the future while remaining anchored to reality. This approach was no doubt better suited to Xerox at that moment, for it was not simply unrealistic, "grandiose thinking." No matter how the exercise is conducted, the point is that at times, and especially in times of trouble, it is important to refocus on the "way out" or on the goal. Mulcahy said this was a turning point, where she personally felt a change in sentiment. She noticed fewer "defections" and more energy and hope.

There are rewards in recognizing values already present in an organization and making sure they remain intact, just as there are rewards to working hard to build values and encouraging employees to participate in the process. With dialogue a priority for Xerox, it is not a coincidence that Xerox employees chose *not* to walk out. The loyalty of its customer base, as well as its employees, meant that they would be there for the company even when times weren't easy. While this period was difficult for Xerox, it will forever serve as a motivational and inspirational example, not only in the event of future challenges.

A key lesson emerging from our study concerns the importance of trust and how it can be built up. Mulcahy's candor with her employees was one of the factors that led them to trust her. Candor, confidence, and trust are key elements of great leadership. This cannot be underscored enough. Sharing information is key. Unless employees are well-informed they cannot be motivated to join the organization's mission. It is incredibly difficult to keep employees involved during challenging times, when they feel insecurity and doubt about the future of their company and their livelihood. Thus candid communication about the state of affairs is a key element to defining how "each employee can help."

By being honest about the state of affairs and displaying confidence, leaders foster in employees a sense of being needed and appreciated. This leads to a sense of belonging and responsibility. As Mulcahy said: "Someone told me soon after I was named president that when times are good you should talk about what needs improvement and when things are bad you should assure people they will get better. I took that advice to heart." She went on to add, "I worried constantly. I had doubts. There were times when the challenges seemed insurmountable. But in public—especially with employees— I was always both candid about our problems and confident we could overcome them. The response was overwhelming. Defections slowed to a trickle. Hope rekindled. Energy returned."

Mulcahy spread the word. Moreover, she made it possible for employees around the world to contribute, too. Such participation by members of the organization can also energize the CEO—it works both ways. Certainly Mulcahy had stores of energy serving her: "In my first year, I did six live television broadcasts for employees, held more than 40 town meetings, sent out more than 20 'letters to the troops,' did hundreds of roundtables, and logged about 100,000 miles visiting employees in more than a dozen countries. And I believe it's fair to say that I've kept that pace up—maybe even intensified it."

By putting intensive effort into communication, the CEOs in our study take advantage of a variety of formats. The remarkable numbers of Mulcahy's spoken and written communications exemplifies the relentlessness necessary to drive key messages home. At the same time, it is not just the quantity but also the quality of words and actions that is important. Mulcahy's candid and confident approach was fruitful:

At the depth of our problems, I gave Xerox people a candid assessment of our problems ... shared with them our strategy to turn Xerox around ... and then gave them a choice—leave Xerox for greener pastures or roll up your sleeves and get to work saving a company we all love. The vast majority chose the latter, "and they were very vocal about why. It's because they all believe they are part of a special company. Most of us joined Xerox in the first place because it stood for something beyond the bottom line, as important as that is.

Xerox people love Xerox. Xerox customers are loyal to Xerox. We wouldn't have survived the past year if we didn't have that love and loyalty. And it stems in some measure from our heritage as a good corporate citizen.

Mulcahy extended her comments to include other companies that can be aligned with Xerox in terms of core values and culture:

So for us—and for all like-minded companies—our past behavior was like money in the bank. It gave us a reservoir of goodwill that we could draw upon in our hour of need. It's so important to us that even in the midst of our financial difficulties, we continued to make grants through The Xerox Foundation. Our employees continued to volunteer in the community. Even as we let people go, we maintained our diversity goals and met our targets. We accelerated our environmental programs and overhauled our governance process.

Effective CEOs remain on the higher road in times of challenge, and Mulcahy's words attest to this: "Although we needed and wanted to turn the company around as quickly as possible, we insisted on doing things right—no corner cutting."

Mulcahy speaks for her entire organization—even beyond her organization when she invokes the participation of her audience, as members of the wider community of people who feel ethics is good for business, or rather, ethics is part of good business.

> You see we all believe that we are part of an ongoing experiment to demonstrate that business success and business ethics are not mutually exclusive. In fact, we believe they are synergistic. There's a lot of tough-minded research around to back that up. A Harvard study, for example, found that companies that balanced the concerns of employees, customers, shareholders and society, grew at four times the rate of companies that focused solely on shareholder value.
>
> That's intuitively true for most of us here today. Our experience at Xerox these past few years bears it out. If employees had voted solely with their checkbooks, they would have left. All we could offer them was hard work, frozen wages, cost cutting, and an uncertain future. But we could offer them one other thing if they were willing to vote with their hearts: the opportunity of a lifetime—the opportunity to save a company that cherished its role in making the world a little better than we found it. It turned out to be a galvanizing force. And they went to work to will Xerox back from the brink of bankruptcy and put it on the road to greatness.

Xerox's return from impending disaster demonstrates the crucial importance of a committed workforce that chooses to persevere and internalize the company's needs. Mulcahy's confidence and candor created buy-in: those who remained really cared about Xerox and believed in the company's success. Ultimately a choice by employees to stick with it resulted in a win-win situation, with Xerox employees contributing to and also reaping the rewards of Xerox's turnaround, not just in monetary terms, but also in being affiliated with a company back "on the road to greatness."

Finally, Mulcahy highlighted the importance of Xerox's roots in helping them weather the storm, a key factor emphasized by many companies we featured. In spite of the difficulties of getting back on the right path, Xerox never abdicated from "doing things right." They never lost the thread of who they were since their founding.

Xerox's "Perfect Storm" was more than a challenge. It provided an ongoing story, a tale of rising to the occasion, a legend of success. It helped define Xerox.

Times of Trial: An Internal Incident

For Pilgrim's Pride Corporation, the challenge came in yet another form. The management of Pilgrim's Pride was shocked to discover an ongoing practice among employees that did not represent the company's ethical stance. Such behaviors, as we established in the Introduction, clearly clashed with the values of the company. "Pilgrim's Pride was founded on ethical principles," said O.B. Goolsby, President and CEO of Pilgrim's Pride Corporation, "and we constantly work hard to do what's right. But, like most large corporations that have been in business for many years, our company has been faced with serious challenges. We believe that our ethical framework—our Guiding Principle, our Core Values, and our integrity—have given us guidance and clarity in our responses to these challenges."

Goolsby described one such challenge, which occurred in July 2004 with the distribution to national media of an "undercover" video showing inhumane treatment of the birds in one of their chicken processing plants. "We were appalled at what we saw in the video," he noted, "and we made it clear that the actions were not in any way condoned by management and were completely contrary to all of our company's practices and policies regarding the humane treatment of poultry."

We can only imagine how this discovery must have felt for the CEO of Pilgrim's Pride, employees, and other stakeholders, too. Their ethics were in question. Their image was at risk. However, determined to stay the course, Pilgrim's Pride relied not only on the rest of their dedicated employees, but also on their personal ethics and morals to correct these unacceptable actions and continue on their path to success.

The importance of strong action is evident in this case. More generally, our analysis has already underlined the value of dedicated employees and a solid foundation.

As soon as management became aware of this video, they immediately took steps to address the allegations of animal abuse. Goolsby explained the company's response: "First, we launched an aggressive and thorough investigation the day we became aware of the video-taped allegations.

"The very next day, we issued a directive to the management team of every Pilgrim's Pride production facility that handles live animals to review our previously-established animal welfare policies and practices in meetings with every employee and supervisor who handles live animals," he recalled. "Managers at all 25 plants stopped production on the current shift and held meetings at the beginning of subsequent shifts to review animal welfare policies and Pilgrim's Pride's zero tolerance for deviations from these policies. We also required signatures from every employee who works with live animals indicating that they reaffirmed their understanding of these policies."

The following day, as a result of their investigation into the violation of their animal welfare policies, Pilgrim's Pride terminated a total of 11 employees. They included one superintendent, one supervisor, one foreman, and eight hourly workers. The company issued this statement to the Associated Press: "Pilgrim's Pride places a high priority on humane treatment of poultry not only because it's the right thing to do, but because it also helps assure high-quality, healthful products for consumers. Pilgrim's Pride's animal welfare policies are designed to eliminate unnecessary harm and suffering to animals in its day-to-day operations."

The company's swift action was dramatic: Managers at all 25 plants stopped production. With the potential for lost sales and profits, this strong move demonstrated just how seriously Pilgrim's Pride took the matter. The decision to interrupt production sent an important message and set an example for the rest of the company. It reinvigorated the ethical behavior of the organization and its employees. The response from Pilgrim's Pride showed a company that does not abdicate from its values ... not even in a tough situation. The company's strong foundation prevailed.

These actions become part of company history, and a story will instruct future generations of employees. Our Introduction considered the importance of such stories in keeping values alive. The experience of Pilgrim's Pride underlines that it is important to remember not only the high points during the life of a corporation. Communicating about difficult moments ensures core values do indeed endure.

Difficult situations also build unity, especially when followed by positive outcomes. Difficult situations also bond participants and onlookers. Like other companies that drew on their ethical foundations to respond to challenges, Pilgrim's Pride weathered its own storm and came out all the stronger.

In summation, Goolsby said: "All in all, we were faced with some disturbing allegations and we had to make some very difficult decisions. But throughout the entire ordeal, we acted quickly and responsibly, and our ethics guided our response. And whenever we are faced with challenges, we rely on our foundation of integrity to always do what we believe is right."

Any number of companies could face a similar plight: discovering an incident that they did not condone as part of their operations. Ethical challenges in certain industries can take on crisis proportions, especially in cases related to the food supply. In any industry, however, sometimes relying on others to carry out directives carries the risk that they might not be carried out in a way that is condoned by management. Sometimes the intention to be unethical isn't really the driving force. Sometimes unethical behavior is born out of a motivation to take a shortcut, to do something more efficiently, and so on. Many companies are similarly vulnerable to such behavior, so it is vital to make a tradition of unwavering values and clear communication.

An Unorthodox Partnership

KeySpan Corporation has had its share of challenges and change. An energy company, it has experienced a number of mergers. During its second-to-last transformation, KeySpan ceased to be Brooklyn Union Gas Co. and went through market deregulation to become the holding company KeySpan. Recently, it was sold to National Grid PLC.

Besides environmental challenges facing companies, mergers bring about much change to an entire organization, often shaking its very foundation. Changes could come about in management, policy, location, name, and reporting relationships. And many other more subtle challenges may ensue.

To help deal with the major change represented by the merger, KeySpan CEO Bob Catell hired Kenny Moore, an ex-monk. Moore's main role was to energize the workforce and bring them closer to Catell, so Catell could better understand their needs. This experience was captured in *The CEO and the Monk: One Company's Journey to Profit and Purpose*,[2] a book Catell and Moore wrote (with Glenn Rifkin) after working together over the years. To offer his views, Catell sent a copy of the book, as well as the DVD of a television program[3] that profiles the duo's unorthodox business partnership.

The unusual team worked together in unusual ways to humanize the organization while facing turbulent times from industry deregulation and a merger.

"KeySpan was in the midst of a gut-wrenching change," the DVD explained. "Like the company's obsolete storage tanks, the energy business as they'd known it was being blown apart and if this 100-year-old gas utility was going to survive, Catell knew it would have

---

[2]Robert B. Catell and Kenny Moore with Glenn Rifkin, *The CEO and the Monk: One Company's Journey to Profit and Purpose*, Hoboken, N.J.: John Wiley & Sons, 2004.
[3]CBS News Sunday Morning, April 11, 2004.

to transform itself." Catell was told, "You were going to have a shock to the system." He replied, "That's correct."

To deal with this major change, Catell hired Kenny Moore. One of six children raised in New York, Moore spent 15 years in a monastic community as a Catholic priest. He gave up his collar and robes only after he became troubled that the church wasn't changing fast enough. He landed a job in the human resources department at Brooklyn Union Gas.

Moore did not know much about business, but this was not an issue for Catell, who stated, "It wasn't really his business acumen that I was looking for; it was his ability to connect with the human side that I was really looking for," adding, "Commitment cannot be mandated to employees. It can only be invited."

From the start, Moore gave radical advice, arguing that change "starts not with a beginning but with an ending." He recalled, "So I said, 'Why don't we do a corporate funeral?' He looked at me like I had two heads." (Catell confirmed his own reaction: "I thought he was crazy.")

In his television appearance, Moore tells the audience that Catell asked him earlier if he could guarantee the corporate funeral would work. Moore's reply was, "of course it's risky, but you are the one saying that we have to go into the future. You are the one saying we have to increase risk-taking." Catell recalled what happened when he tried to convince the other officers in the company: "They were a little skeptical . . . they even thought I was crazy—but it worked."

Four hundred KeySpan executives were invited to the service, paying their respects to the past, but also looking to the future. Catell explained: "Then we used those 400 or so people in the room to be,

I guess, sort of apostles to go out and talk to the rest of the employees about the need for this change."

Moore emphasized the value of the strong message sent by Catell: "For him to take that risk, I think it gave permission to our other corporate leaders to go and do likewise. I think it also telegraphed to our employees that they were not alone, that the CEO was willing to be vulnerable."

The way Catell and Moore spoke about the "corporate funeral" underlines that an important part of moving forward for KeySpan was saying goodbye to the past and accepting the distinctly different challenges of the future. What Kenny Moore brought to the table was an organized way to do that. We have seen in other cases that giving names to problems or events makes them easier to relegate to the past after they are resolved. In the case of KeySpan, a highly symbolic moment was organized. This approach was particular to KeySpan and appropriate for the company's needs at that moment. It also allowed other KeySpan leaders to accept their vulnerability in managing the turbulent times and to believe that doing their best and taking risks would help them move forward.

The success of the funeral cemented Catell and Moore's relationship. It also increased Catell's confidence in Moore, who encouraged him to come down from the executive floor to rally his employees. Moore was an important catalyst in encouraging Catell to take the time to personalize his relationship with his employees.

Moore had more unusual suggestions for Catell, including bringing a graphic artist into the KeySpan cafeteria to help executives sketch out a mural of how they envisioned the future of the company. He also brought an improvisational comedian in to help teach ad-libbing skills. Catell reflected on the experience: "I admit I even had some trouble participating in the session when I did it, and I kind of made a little bit of a fool of myself. But maybe that was part of what we were trying to do here: to show our employees that none of us are perfect."

Acting on Moore's suggestions, Catell's approach to humanizing the organization was not only unique but effective. His experiment helped executives find a creative way to unfetter their thinking while taking a constructive step toward their visions for the future. It allowed them to construct a collective, unified vision. Doing so in an open arena helped secure visual reinforcement for the progress, which involved each participant.

The approach to change at KeySpan was crucial in helping employees feel secure during the change process. It was also effective in helping them loosen up and use turbulence to build a stronger new mindset and new vision for the future of KeySpan.

Transforming a Traditional, Regulated Utility

Peter A. Darbee, CEO of Pacific Gas and Electric Company (PG&E), describes the moral compass that guided efforts "intended to transform a traditional, regulated utility toward a high-performance, competitive enterprise." He wrote to us about his views on ethics and ethics-related initiatives. He also included a DVD that features him addressing his employees at an offsite, multiday corporate conference. "These offsites are integral to the transformation of our company," wrote Darbee.

Darbee described the magnitude of the challenge and affirmed his confidence that their efforts would be fruitful: "It is a vast undertaking, with a company of 20,000 employees, 100 years of heritage, and over $30 billion of assets. Nevertheless, while we believe that the entire effort will take a full three to five years, we are confident that we will achieve this result. We are equally certain that we'll only achieve this result if we keep our full attention on integrity, open and honest communication, a passion for customer needs, as well as delivering for our shareholders. Fundamental to our approach needs to be a deeply-rooted respect for each other and an attitude of not only tolerating our diversity but celebrating it."

Darbee stressed responsibility and accountability, saying, "We recognize that we must be accountable for our actions, safety of employees, and protection of the environment and supporting our communities. We know that we will only be able to achieve this if we act as a team and are committed to excellence and innovation." PG&E's commitment has served the environment and communities well. For the past 25 years, the company has led various bird species conservation initiatives and is a member of joint ventures that serve to protect, restore, increase, and enhance all types of wetlands. In recognition of its ongoing, industry-leading avian protection efforts, it received Audubon California's first ever Corporate Achievement Award in 2008.[4] In addition, PG&E, along with the National Fish and Wildlife Foundation, is also part of the Nature Restoration Trust, which awards grants to community organizations to foster stewardship of California's diverse wildlife and habitats. The Nature

---

[4]http://www.pge.com/about/news/mediarelations/newsreleases/q2_2008/080513.shtml.

Restoration Trust has invested over $2 million in projects to conserve and enhance wildlife in their habitats.[5]

The DVD shows Darbee carefully communicating to employees the ethical obligations that PG&E has toward its stakeholders and how far-reaching these obligations are. He presents accountability to the customer as equivalent to holding your head up in the community.

Peter Darbee's attempt to broaden the ownership of responsibility and accountability to the collective is an effort to help ensure that attention to doing what is right—in this case for the customer—remain of utmost importance to every PG&E employee. In centering attention on each customer, the totality of PG&E's efforts, not just the efforts of a single department, affects the overall community.

In his presentation, Darbee describes a call from an old friend about electricity and gas having been turned off in an apartment. A lapse in customer service, for a business that provides gas and electricity to the community, has a direct effect on the customer. A small gap in the web of customer-service representatives can allow a customer solution to be unattended. Although the company and its representatives had intended to serve the customer, one story describes a challenge. Darbee dissects the narrative and what happened as a way to discuss how PG&E can be more customer focused.

"We are accountable for all of our actions," Darbee tells viewers. "These include safely protecting the environment and supporting our communities." In one scenario, he outlines an interpretation of accountability that he considers too limited: equating accountability with adequate performance of one's job. Darbee tells employees that

---

[5]http://www.pge.com/about/news/mediarelations/newsreleases/q2_2008/080529.shtml.

accountability is a broader concept than the way it is often traditionally identified. "Accountability," he says, "is an organizational account-ability. Obviously, we first need to do the job that's in front of us, but we have to think about the entire organization."

Darbee's emphasis on increasing accountability and bringing it to each individual in the organization is an important way for PG&E to meet its challenges and obligations to its customers, share-holders, and other stakeholders. His discussion of accountability speaks to the environment and shows how the challenge in gas and electrical utilities is to meet customer needs as an organization. In this regard, all service organizations face the challenge of attending to customers and recognizing when something in the organization needs to change.

Darbee underlines the importance of working as a team, rather than as a utility finance group, a corporate finance group, a new construction versus division, and so on: "What we really need to do is recognize that there is one PG&E and our job is about serving the customers. We can't let these divisions get in the way." He continues, "So not only do we have to work as a team, we also have to protect our environment. We can hold our head up in our community only if we're being a leader in protecting our environment."

Ethics, especially in customer service, should not succumb to an organizational structure that allows for excuses like "the other department is responsible for this" or "this is not our territory." Darbee clarifies that ethics and the greater challenge of serving customers day to day is a "company" job—"our job." He also stresses the overall responsibility to the environment and defines the individual employee's job as having a much wider-ranging impact than that of a "customer service rep." Instead, each person in the company represents a key element that contributes to PG&E completing its environmental mission and contribution.

We've seen how CEOs use stories to help keep values alive. We've also seen how they meet challenges, using them to galvanize employees and encourage a culture of ethics. In Chapter 3 we'll examine how CEOs and their corporations are using a range of concrete measures—from written codes to interactive initiatives—to encourage ethical behavior and integrity.

Chapter 3

Taking Tangible Steps to Harness Ethical Energy

CODES OF CONDUCT and ethics statements act as a formal foundation. They are the fundamental building blocks for going beyond mere compliance. Their real value, however, is in the way companies make them come alive for employees. This is a key point: Companies intent on building a climate of ethics bring the codes home to employees by involving them in a range of initiatives. The CEO must take an active role in this process. The most effective codes are visually prominent and carefully articulated, but this is not enough. Ethically alert organizations know this. They make efforts to ensure attention to the codes and to motivate employees to enact the codes and make them part of their everyday activities.

The companies in our study use mixed modes to capture the attention and enthusiasm of employees, with dialogue often backing up written statements. Through code-related activities, each company makes the code specific to the organization and helps build what could be called "ethical capital." Indeed, companies recognize ethics as capital and are constantly building and expanding its reach.

They recognize the importance of previously held ethical stock and the necessity to accumulate more ethical capital for the entire community of stakeholders.

The companies in our study ensure that employees, colleagues, managers, and officers understand the codes and interpret them correctly. In the design of codes and handbooks, the strategic use of language plays a role, but there is more to it than that. CEOs and their companies stoke employee enthusiasm about what the codes mean for the organization's overall success. They link the necessity for ethical behavior with the organization's prosperity. They allow employees to be accountable and responsible, giving them a personal stake to make a personal difference. The codes are intertwined with job satisfaction and professionalism.

The written codes and related initiatives we examined also share a more intangible quality: they suggest an evolutionary nature of ethics in some companies. Ethics is not at all a static concept. Initiatives are ongoing, with many of the companies revisiting their codes yearly and allowing employees to interpret the codes through open dialogues via hotlines or corporate forums. Written texts use language in a way that can more easily involve readers, and readership can extend beyond internal audiences through the availability of ethics materials and archives on corporate Web sites. Companies edit, build, and adapt codes and initiatives to changing challenges and times.

By necessity, then, the codes, statements, and initiatives discussed in this and other chapters are a snapshot in time—one that is worth examining. As much as codes and initiatives need to evolve to fit new situations, core foundations do not change: Ethics is timeless. Vintage ethics and ethical archives are present as part of this foundation and are poised for further development.

Our study underlines the meticulous approach companies take toward written corporate materials such as vision statements, codes of conduct, and codes of ethics. The sheer variety of tangible initiatives—from ethics programs, training sessions, and meetings to special tools and events—shows how each company makes an effort to customize its written code, making it specific to the organization and thus building ethical capital.

Previous chapters have underlined the role of stories, involvement, and dialogue in encouraging a culture of ethics. Now we'll see how CEOs and their corporations are working relentlessly on a range of concrete measures—from written codes to interactive initiatives—to encourage integrity and harness ethical energy.

Systems of Concrete Measures Aligning with Values

In Chapter 1, Richard A. Goldstein, CEO of International Flavors & Fragrances (IFF), shared his views on three key elements to being an ethical company: leadership, values, and systems. The third element, "systems," represents concrete measures. There are a number of tools that IFF has put in place to clarify and enforce their position on ethical behavior.

The corporations in our study give ongoing attention to ethics, and IFF exemplifies this. The company has a 20-page Code of Business Conduct and Ethics that covers health, safety, and environmental issues; sexual harassment and equal opportunity employment; intellectual property protection; and competition and antitrust policies. According to Goldstein, managers and officers are required to read and sign the Code of Conduct once a year. IFF has multiple avenues for reporting violations or suspected violations, including e-mail boxes and telephone numbers of officers and independent directors. The Code of Conduct is available online and in print, and key messages from it are reinforced in the company's employee handbook and throughout their Web site.

The company's initiatives are perpetual and evolutionary—not stagnant, forgotten, or even stale. The annual attention to codes, for example, is an important symbol to employees. Actions taken on a yearly basis, such as signing the Code of Conduct, build employees' ethical awareness. IFF's comprehensive Code of Conduct is also widely distributed. Furthermore, IFF demonstrates its strong support for the code and an intense effort to encourage adherence by providing venues for the vigilant to report those who stray.

Goldstein underscored the importance of aligning systems with values. "One system that absolutely must be aligned with a company's values and ethical standards is its rewards system," he said. "If a company's values statement says that product quality is paramount, but an individual manager constantly recognizes and promotes the team members who focus only on low-cost production at the expense of quality, his department will be confused at best. At worst, that company's customers and corporate reputation can be put in grave danger."

Effective organizations do not send mixed messages. The example cited by Goldstein highlights an important point: effective organizations know it's a mistake to reward *A* while hoping for *B*. Effective organizations do not reward, for example, cost-cutting measures *at any price*, while *hoping* employees do not take measures that would sacrifice ethics. Messages need to be aligned with values.

Goldstein turned his attention to the board: "Finally, it goes without saying that a company's Board of Directors plays an absolutely critical role in corporate governance," he affirmed. "All boards—including IFF's—have become much more active in the past couple of years, and they take their oversight role very seriously, as they should. Having a strong, experienced, and independent board is more important than ever, and I welcome and encourage our board's involvement, diligence, and even its occasional criticism." Goldstein thus reinforces IFF's transparency and signaled that the door is open to involvement and input from the outside.

Showing Commitment to Integrity and Helping People Make Ethical Decisions

From Day One, communicating the importance of integrity was paramount to Hospira. In the Introduction, we saw how Hospira embraced the opportunity to create an organization built on integrity. Christopher B. Begley, chairman and CEO, talked about the first tangible steps the company took. "To drive home our company's commitment to integrity, one of the first things we did for our Hospira colleagues was identify a book called *The Integrity Advantage: How Taking the High Road Creates a Competitive Advantage in Business*,[1] which really spells out why integrity is so critical to both individuals' and an organization's success," he said. "We gave it to all of our employees the day the company launched. We also used it to help develop our Code of Business Conduct, an informative booklet that covers eight principles of integrity."

---

[1]Adrian Gostick and Dana Telford, *The Integrity Advantage*, Salt Lake City: Gibbs Smith, 2003.

The simple act of sharing a book with all employees shows how Hospira took no chances in ensuring that all employees reach a common understanding. Using a common base and foundation for statements like Hospira's Code of Business Conduct is an important step toward making such codes a living, active part of the organization.

Begley described Hospira's initiative in detail. "The Code spells out integrity in simple language,—*languages*, really, because we issued it in several languages to reach our global population. After making sure that each Hospira employee and contractor received a copy of the Code, we explained it in live, face-to-face training sessions all over the world," he said. "Finally, we followed up with a short test and a certification that employees and contractors are required to sign. Each new employee and contractor that joins Hospira is required to complete these tasks as well."

Our study highlights the way multiple modes work together. In the case of Hospira, the company also goes the extra mile in having personalized training sessions to reach employees operating in different locations and, more importantly, different cultures. The company makes sure that ethics is not lost in translation. By using the most comprehensive personal form of communication, Hospira ensures the message is not diluted. The personal approach increases accountability.

At the same time, Hospira launched an awareness campaign to make sure their employees knew about the company's Ethics and Compliance Hotline. Begley said, "We wanted them to know they could report any concerns or questions in a way that would protect their identity, and that we would investigate and respond to those concerns in a fair and timely way. In doing all this, we weren't trying to teach our employees to snitch on one another, and we weren't teaching them rules or laws. We were trying to show them how serious we are about integrity, and we were trying to teach them certain principles, and thereby give them a moral compass that will help them make ethical decisions."

Like other organizations intent on nurturing a climate of ethics, Hospira communicates its values and its attention to ethics not only by having a venue where employees can report oversights, but also by allowing those with questions or concerns to discuss their dilemmas via a hotline. This important outlet ensures a constant ethical dialogue. Employees who do not want to draw too much attention to a situation can still discuss it and get feedback. This outlet for active participation also helps keep enthusiasm high at Hospira—something Begley recognizes as key. Active participation keeps ethics alive and evolving in each employee. Employees are able to discuss and draw on the codes to meet the challenges of diverse situations as they emerge. The hotline allows room for interpretation even when employees are challenged by a not-so-clear situation that doesn't fall neatly into a set of existing codes.

Begley admits his worries—and his awareness that the advantages of being a new company require work to flourish. "Several years following the launch of our new company, what continues to keep me up at night is the notion that one day the novelty of our new culture will wear off," he said. "I know that unless we work hard to sustain the enthusiasm, it will likely burn out. So we are continuously working on ways to deepen our employees' emotional attachment to our evolving culture, and to help instill a lasting passion."

Culture-Building Fun...

Begley described more of the ways the company helps maintain the novelty, deepen emotions, and instill passion. "For instance, during the last two Olympic Games, we held our own Hospira Olympics—where the competition was not about athletics, but about highlighting individual stories and images that depict Hospira's commitment to our stakeholders and our values," he explained. "For the two competitions, we received thousands of entries from Hospira employees all over the world, and gave out gold, silver and bronze medals to winners at multiple sites."

Begley stressed the importance of fun: "This may sound like a lot of fun and games—and I think it should—because I believe that fun should be a part of life in the workplace. In fact, at Hospira we have a team dedicated to making fun a part of the fabric of our lives— coming up with creative and interactive ways to reinforce Hospira's vision, values, and commitment."

In analyzing Hospira's materials, we were struck by its creativity. What better way to build ethical energy and dedication to corporate success than building fun into the workplace? Hospira places much value on fun and personally reaching each employee through culture-building activities.

Begley stressed that this approach to cultural values is a key element in determining the company's success. "As an organization, Hospira has core competencies in three key areas that are critical to our customers. Our products help improve productivity, increase patient and caregiver safety, and reduce costs. So far we have succeeded and I am confident that we will continue to deliver on our customers' needs in those areas. However, our ability to drive the company culture with our vision, values, and commitment as the core will be key to the longevity of our success.

"Integrity, accountability/ownership, entrepreneurial spirit, and speed—Hospira continues to work hard to inculcate these four cultural values into our organization," he observed. "With the challenges facing business today, it is vital to keep ethics front and center in the minds of our business leaders. Embracing integrity and focusing on business ethics are key ways that an individual can positively differentiate themselves both personally and professionally."

Begley's statements highlight that Hospira's active approach to focusing on integrity and ethics brings these values as close to the core of the company's culture as strategic planning and other necessary functions. Engendering employee attention to its core values and fostering personal ties to Hospira can only help the company's success in the eyes of all stakeholders. It is a strategy that fosters long-term gains.

"From Hospira's point of view, our emphasis on integrity has been integral to our cultural progress to date. The working environment we are nurturing continues to motivate our employees to be engaged, excited and productive," Begley concluded. "We have consistently provided solid returns to shareholders. We are establishing Hospira as an employer and global citizen of choice in the communities in which we do business. And most importantly, we continue to deliver on our business strategy in a way that holds integrity in the highest regard and ensures that we live up to the most basic principle of integrity: delivering on our promises."

Our Vision[2]

Advancing Wellness...
Through the right people and the right products.

---

[2]The text is from the company's artwork on the Hospira vision, and the visual element is not reproduced here.

Our Commitment

Hospira has an unwavering commitment to:

Our customers, delivering on our promise by serving their needs with integrity and trust.

Our employees, by embracing diversity of thought and cultural perspective, and fostering an environment of empowerment, fairness, and respect.

Our shareholders, by safeguarding their investment and providing a fair return.

Our communities, acknowledging our social responsibility through active citizenship and thoughtful giving.

Our Values

We will achieve our vision and deliver on our commitment through:

Integrity: We build respect and trust in our company, products, and selves by setting high standards and acting on our values.

Ownership/Accountability: You are the heart and soul of our company. Your words and actions determine our reputation. As an owner of our company, you are counted on to advance our performance by meeting your commitments and keeping your promises.

Speed: You are empowered and expected to act quickly and decisively in everything you do while making informed decisions and ethical judgments.

Entrepreneurial Spirit: We respect and encourage visionary thinking by embracing people who are passionate champions of creative ideas and who are willing to persevere on behalf of innovation.

Doing the Right Thing—Always

A key challenge in encouraging ethical behavior is the broad room for interpretation when complex multi-faceted situations are not addressed by pre-specified codes of behavior—even those that are specific to a company's business. We've already underlined the importance of written documents, which act as a formal foundation. Codes are not limited to internal initiatives, but are also part of companies' ethics-related efforts that are broadcast to other audiences on corporate Web sites or in printed materials.

It is worthwhile to zoom in on excerpts from company documents to dissect how they build a climate of ethics where each individual is part of an organizational effort and knows where to turn for guidance. Clarity is foremost, and well-chosen words can strengthen key messages and the organization's ethical voice. Let's take the example of ITT and its code of conduct, which is introduced by CEO Steve Loranger.

The *Code of Corporate Conduct* is subtitled *Doing the Right Thing—Always*. The code's title makes a powerful statement about the company's stance right from the start. The use of "always" leaves no room for doubt. The strength of the message is also clear in the words of Loranger in the "Letter from the CEO," which opens the document. Any gray areas are then diminished within its 41 pages, with information and examples easily retrieved thanks to a detailed table of contents. Different styles are used, including anecdotes representing hypothetical cases that are part of everyday life, with questions representing additional styles.

The Letter from the CEO sends key messages not only by language, but also by format, spacing, sentence length, and paragraph organization. Loranger expresses the need for a uniform vision for ethics—called a "beacon"—to guide each employee. The emphasis on values stands out in a one-sentence paragraph in the middle of the foreword: "ITT's values define us as a company."

Longer paragraphs are interspersed with short sentences for high impact: a longer sentence elaborating on what "we may be tempted" to do is punctuated by a terse five-word statement: "We do not do it." Repetition drives home the message in the next sentence: "If there is any question, any question at all about the ethics or legality of a deal, I do not want the business."

> To navigate on any journey, you need a beacon to guide you, a travel plan to show you the way. The need is no different when guiding a large, global corporation. With people and facilities around the world, it is critical that the company have uniform standards that everyone knows and follows. At ITT the Code of Corporate Conduct serves as our beacon.
>
> Please take time to read and become familiar with the ITT Code of Corporate Conduct. As CEO, I personally hold myself and each of the leaders who report to me responsible to these standards every day. Accountability, integrity, and respect are central to our Management System. Refer to our values when making decisions. Integrate them into meetings and team activities. Support people doing the right thing. Encourage each other in your words and actions to rise to the highest standards of ethical behavior.
>
> ITT's values define us as a company.
>
> ITT expects every employee, consultant, marketing representative, and sales agent—whatever their position, and wherever

they may be in the world—to do the right thing always. There are times when we may be tempted to push the edge or bend the rules to make a special commitment for a customer, or otherwise make an exception to get the job done. We do not do it. If there is any question, any question at all about the ethics or legality of a deal, I do not want the business. I expect each ITT employee to feel the same, regardless of pressures to deliver financial results.

I am proud to work with people who take such pride in their company's ethical culture. It takes years to build this kind of trust, but only moments to destroy it. Our commitment to living our values day in and day out is vital to our success, and is one of the reasons that I believe ITT will continue to be a great company for years to come. Please join me in reaffirming that pledge.

Steve Loranger
Chairman, President and
Chief Executive Officer

The all-inclusiveness in the second paragraph also stands out: everyone is accountable. The CEO holds himself accountable to the exact same standards he expects his direct reports and employees to uphold. More "all-inclusiveness" characterizes the fourth paragraph through the use of *we* and lists of positions representing people who are accountable, *whatever* the position and *wherever* in the world they are.

The Overview section to the Code of Corporate Conduct urges employees to ask for help when in doubt: "Where conflicts exist with local policy or regulations, the requirement containing the higher standard of ethical conduct shall apply." That is followed by another statement in larger typeface: "If you have any doubt, ask for help."

The Table of Contents shows that the document covers many areas: core ethical values; ethical decision making; points of contact; accuracy of records; antitrust; business courtesies; conflicts of interest and corporate opportunities; consultants; e-mail, Internet, and information technology.

The *Core Ethical Values* section repeats the word "always," reinforcing the company's stance on ethics: ITT is committed to doing the right thing always. Not only time ("always") but also space is addressed in building an ethical climate. "Our values are all around us: they are intrinsic to the ITT work environment, they give us strength, they sustain our vitality. At ITT ethics is in the air we breathe," Loranger said. Some of the values important to ITT are described: accountability/responsibility, diversity, fairness, good citizenship, honesty/truthfulness, inclusion, integrity, quality, and respect.

The variety of styles and approaches incorporated into the Code make it more likely to reach people with different preferences and learning styles. Its section on ethical decision making includes a descriptive section as well as a list of five questions to help employees determine whether their actions are proper. They include: Would I want my actions reported on the front page of a newspaper? What would my family, friends, or neighbors think of my actions?

The section ends reiterating the importance of asking when in doubt: "if you remain uncertain about what to do, stop and ask for help. Refer to the relevant section of this Code. Speak with your supervisor or, if you prefer, communicate with any of the other points of contact indicated in this Code." These alternatives remind the employee that at times behaving ethically means asking about doubts and not necessarily trying to resolve one's doubts without guidance. The organization is there to support the individual, whose choices include asking for help. The individual in turn supports the organization.

Though many points of interest stand out, the final one we have chosen concerns the Frequently Asked Questions (FAQ) included in each section of the code. Anecdotes are designed to represent dilemmas and doubts that may present themselves in everyday situations. One example is a FAQ in the Code's section on antitrust: the personal and the professional overlap with an employee socializing with a friend from a competing firm.

> At a trade association meeting, I played golf with a Vice President from a competing firm. We are old friends from college. While sitting in the cart, we started talking about how business was going. He indicated that his firm was looking very closely at raising prices next month. I quickly broke in and said that I did not think it was appropriate to be discussing that sort of information. Since we had just finished the last hole, I returned to my hotel room and left a message for someone in our Company Legal Department to call me. Now I am thinking that I was too quick to act. After all, everything was very informal. What do you think? Was I too harsh on my friend?

A: You did the right things. Even informal discussions among competitors about price may be potential antitrust violations with possible criminal penalties. When you speak to the Company Legal Department explain exactly what happened.

The first-person account underscores how natural it is to feel unsure in a casual setting. A friendly conversation with an old friend during a golf game may have made it seem natural to discuss business, but the employee's reaction—to cut off the discussion—was the right one. As the reply indicates, even an informal discussion about price may be an antitrust violation. The admonishment to ask when in doubt is reinforced here and elsewhere in the document.

Other examples are more direct. A situation arises and creates a doubt: what should I do? The reply is straight to the point and the reader is reminded of the important role of the Company Legal Department.

Q: I received a fax today. The cover sheet leads me to believe that the attached pages were misdirected and contain a competitor's proposal. What is the right thing to do?
A: Do not look at the attached pages. Do not copy the document. Contact your Company Legal Department immediately.

These and other FAQs and responses increase employees' understanding of ethical behavior by providing concrete examples in clear, direct, and plain language. The approach reassures them that it is natural to have doubts. Two key areas of the codes are salient: the idea of "always," which underlines the company's unwavering ethical stance, and the instruction "when in doubt seek advice," which puts the organization in a supportive role and reduces the risk of violations.

A Multi-Pronged Approach

Xerox Corporation uses what they call the five-pronged approach to social responsibility and business ethics. These five planks also form Xerox's nucleus program. Anne M. Mulcahy, Chairman and CEO of Xerox Corporation, described the approach: "First, we take environmental management very seriously. Before it was popular to do so—more than two decades ago—Xerox adopted a policy that protects the environment and the health and safety of our employees, customers, and neighbors. This principle is central to the way Xerox does business in every nation around the globe. We articulate our environmental goal in just a few words: making Waste-Free Products in Waste-Free Factories to help our customers attain Waste-Free Workplaces." She added, "Last year, we diverted nearly 160 million pounds of waste from landfills, recycled 85 percent of our nonhazardous solid waste, and promulgated tough standards for our paper suppliers.

"Second, we have overhauled and strengthened our governance process," continued Mulcahy. "We've aggressively embraced Sarbanes-Oxley; promulgated a new Code of Ethics; trained and retrained all our people on their responsibilities; given employees an easy and anonymous vehicle to raise issues; and enabled our Board to be more independent and involved in governance of the company.

"We treat good business ethics as everyone's responsibility," she said. "People know what's expected of them. They know how to raise issues. And we have a world-class process in place to ensure that every concern is examined thoroughly. If we find a problem, we fix it."

We can see that Xerox has a very circumspect ethical approach, with its Code of Ethics serving as a foundation, supplemented by training and opportunities for employees to be involved in discussing issues. In our study, we found the use of multiple modes—written codes as a foundation combined with other initiatives—to be important. This example shows how Xerox allows the individual to assert responsibility for overall corporate ethics through its multi-pronged approach.

"The third plank of our program is corporate philanthropy, spearheaded by The Xerox Foundation. We invest about $15 million a year in nonprofit organizations—and I use the word 'invest' deliberately," she continued. "We don't write a check and walk away. We consider our donations to be investments in improving the organization's capacity to positively impact the quality of life in the community in some tangible, measurable way. We support some 400 organizations each year and in about 80 percent of the cases a Xerox person is personally involved. They are either board members or volunteers or serve in some other capacity. We find that this synergy between Xerox money and Xerox people ensures a greater return on our investment."

This is a good example of going beyond compliance, a key point that emerges from our study. Xerox also sees its responsibility as reaching outward to "invest" in communities, where they remain involved. It helps their investments grow and in return develops their human resources—their employees.

"Fourth, we encourage volunteerism at the grassroots level. Last year, some fifteen thousand employees in the United States alone participated in the affairs of their communities under the auspices of Xerox," Mulcahy continued. "One example: in Rochester, New York, a group of Xerox Lean Six Sigma Black Belts are helping eight community organizations improve their business processes, boost productivity and improve client satisfaction." [Lean Six Sigma is a methodology that streamlines businesses for greater efficiency.]

"There are other outlets for the volunteer spirit of our people as well," she explained. "Xerox employees contributed more than \$2 million last year to United Way campaigns across the country. They served on thousands of non-profit boards. They held public office. They participated in our Social Service Leave Program which allows a select group of Xerox people to serve in the community for periods as long as a year at full pay."

We found numerous examples of how companies in our study help build values in the workplace. One of the ways Xerox does this is by "lending" its human resources to the community. It gives back human capital in all areas of diverse communities, which also receive financial aid from employee contributions.

Mulcahy concluded with the final plank of the program: "And, of course, the fifth prong of our social responsibility strategy is a relentless focus on diversity. We treat it as a line responsibility—not as something 'nice to do' but as a business imperative that you must do to remain competitive. Senior managers throughout the company are evaluated on their performance in hiring and promoting what we call a balanced workforce. Each operating unit is given short-term and long-term staffing goals. We inspect progress regularly as part of our normal business reviews.

"We have a variety of programs around flex-time and job-sharing and day-care and elder care," she concludes. "When we're forced to downsize, we expect and insist that the job reductions mirror our balanced workforce targets. We include diversity in our statement of core values and communicate its importance often and consistently."

Mulcahy underlines a key feature of Xerox's business ethics program: "Taken one by one, they are hardly unique. Most progressive companies today have similar programs. Where I believe we may have some unique advantages is that we have been pursuing these strategies for a very long time and we have integrated them into the way we run Xerox. They are not stand-alone, nice-to-do initiatives. They are part and parcel of our management process, our culture, our DNA. As we like to say, they are part of what makes Xerox, Xerox."

Xerox's long-standing approach to ethics gives the company ethical capital not in a point-in-time measurement but rather in a trajectory of knowledge, know-how, and process. It is second nature for their employees, whose development is shaped through these experiences, to bring them back into their work. This approach allows employees to develop their ethical awareness. Each employee's individual contributions in the areas of the five planks build Xerox's strong ethical stance. Xerox's multi-pronged approach to ethics is a self-reinforcing construct that is evolutionary and ongoing.

Core Values, the Company and the Community

O.B. Goolsby, former President and CEO of Pilgrim's Pride Corporation, also underscored the importance of defining and communicating values from the company's inception and articulating them in writing. "Pilgrim's Pride Corporation is guided by what you might refer to as our 'moral compass'—a set of values that have defined us since day one," he explained. "But these values are more than just ideas; they are written statements—our Core Values—that are the foundation of everything we do."

Below is a section from the handbook for Pilgrim's Pride Corporation employees, who are referred to as "our Partners" by the company:

Pilgrim's Pride Core Values

At Pilgrim's Pride, our Core Values are our foundation.
Our values guide us in our daily decisions and dictate our overall business strategy.
　Our guiding principle will be The Golden Rule:

"However you want people to treat you, so treat them."

Our Integrity

We will strive to be a company of people known for integrity in all of our dealings. The basis of our decisions will be doing what is right, not just in terms of that which is technically correct, but by doing that which is just, fair, and equitable in light of the circumstances.
　We will deal honestly and non-deceptively, with our word as our bond and expect reciprocity; living up to the spirit, not just the letter of the law.

Goolsby's words remind us of how important people are and of how closely people are linked to success. "We strongly believe that our success is largely dependent on the way we treat people—our Partners, our customers, our suppliers, the family farmers who grow poultry under contract for our company, and the people in the communities in which we live and work. This drives our day-to-day activities at Pilgrim's Pride and is the focus of everything we do."

Our analysis of materials highlights the great care Pilgrim's Pride takes in protecting and building its ethical archives, carefully documenting their core foundation from its inception. In so doing it includes the elements key to its ethical success: stakeholders such as employees, customers, suppliers, and farmers. Pilgrim's Pride has a stake in all of their actions since they have a stake in the actions of Pilgrim's Pride. Its strong sense of reciprocity is a driving force behind its ethical continuity.

Pilgrim's Pride has established a Code of Conduct and Ethics to spell out what is expected of all employees and officers of the company. This document is published on the company's Web site,[3] and covers in detail such topics as compliance with laws, rules and regulations, insider trading, conflicts of interest, confidentiality, fair dealing, and accountability. Here, too, we see the importance of using multiple approaches and providing alternative, confidential, outlets.

"In addition to our Code of Conduct and Ethics, we maintain a confidential, toll-free hotline that we call The PRIDE Line, which is available 24 hours a day, seven days a week to allow our Partners to report any situations that might cause harm to Pilgrim's Pride or to our Partners," explained Goolsby. "We encourage any Partner,

---

[3]The Code is available at: http://www.pilgrimspride.com/investors/codeofconduct.aspx.

vendor, or grower who is aware of unethical or inappropriate behavior in the workplace to call The PRIDE Line. Examples of behaviors that might be reported include theft or embezzlement, conflicts of interest, violation of SEC laws or regulations, fraud, sexual harassment, workplace violence or threat of violence, workplace drug use, safety issues, or violations of company policies."

To make all of its Partners aware of this resource, Pilgrim's Pride created a brochure explaining The PRIDE Line and how to use it, which they distributed to its then 40,000 Partners in the United States (including Puerto Rico) and Mexico. In addition, the company widely publicizes the PRIDE Line's toll-free numbers on an ongoing basis, including them in every issue of their corporate newsletter and posting them on bulletin boards in their facilities company-wide. As Goolsby noted, "this is just another example of 'walking the talk'—making sure we back up our ethical standards and expectations with action."

Similar to other companies in our study, Pilgrim's Pride acts so that employees feel welcome to come forward and also feel protected in curtailing non-ethical behavior. Pilgrim's Pride has specific practices that underlie their ethical principles.

Goolsby brought up another example of how the company's aims go beyond what may be expected in terms of ethical initiatives: "One of the programs we have established, which we believe is rather unique among Fortune 500 companies, is Pilgrim's Cares, a confidential and comprehensive employee care program that is offered nationwide to all our Partners. Under this program, chaplains are available to our Partners nationwide, 24 hours a day, 365 days a year for crisis intervention and emergency situations." Goolsby specified that these services are provided as a benefit at no cost to the company's Partners and their family members, and are completely voluntary and confidential. Pilgrim's Cares chaplains are not company employees, and the service is not a part of Pilgrim's Pride operations.

Services offered by the Pilgrim's Cares program include regular, brief worksite visits as well as hospital, nursing home, funeral home, family home, and other neutral site visits, when appropriate. The program also provides chaplains for confidential individual and immediate family discussions of personal issues including marriage, divorce and remarriage, serious illness, death and grief recovery, child rearing, care of aging parents, or other concerns. It also makes a referral service available and coordinates specialized assistance for Partners and/or immediate family members with specific needs.

"We believe that in showing our employees that we care about their family concerns and spiritual life as well as their workplace issues," said Goolsby, "we help build bridges of trust that, we hope, lead to a more caring, concerned, and ethical workforce."

We can see that hand in hand with its emphasis on reciprocity, Pilgrim's Pride takes great effort in caring for its employees and instituting corporate care. Its corporate stewardship encompasses its own employees, offering them personalized care during employees' most difficult personal situations. Thus, Pilgrim's Pride ensures an unprecedented level of reciprocity with its employees, which helps Pilgrim's Pride earn their loyalty and ethical vigilance.

Pilgrim's Pride also has an eye toward the community. Goolsby observed that being an ethical company also means being a good corporate citizen. "To Pilgrim's Pride, this means giving back to the communities in which we live and work," he said. "Our Partners contribute to their towns and neighborhoods in almost every way imaginable, from adopting stretches of highway and supporting local schools to sponsoring holiday toy drives, participating in walkathons and coaching youth sports teams."

This commitment, said Goolsby, reflects the company's origins in small-town America: "The traditional values of warmth, courtesy, pride and a willingness to pitch in and help those in need defines the company's spirit, whether in big cities like Dallas or Phoenix or in communities like Center, Texas, and Enterprise, Alabama."

Just as important are the company's contributions to the economic health of the communities in the 18 states in which their Partners live and work, said Goolsby. He pointed out that the vast majority of their 40,000 employees live in small towns: "We know that jobs that provide regular hours, full benefits, pay scales that exceed minimum wage, and good opportunities for advancement are not always easy to find outside of major business centers, so we realize that our company is an integral part the overall economic health of many small communities," he noted. "We understand that when the community and its people benefit, the company and its stakeholders do, too, and we take the responsibility of being a good corporate citizen very seriously."

Also of great importance is the protection and preservation of the vital land and water resources in these communities. Chairman Bo Pilgrim has set forth his vision of environmental stewardship in this statement:

The Purpose of Pilgrim's Pride Corporation is, within God's Will, to help save Rural North America and the Family Farms in the United States, Mexico and Puerto Rico, by the creation of jobs through the production of healthy, nutritious and economical chicken, turkey, and egg products for the rest of the world.

It is our commitment to seek to protect and enhance God's environmental resources through the use of the best affordable and practical science, technology and animal welfare practices available for use in the agriculture industry. By applying these industry best management practices to our uses of land, water, and air resources, we will operate within local, state and federal rules and regulations and demonstrate our commitment toward environmental stewardship.

We will always give God the credit for our progress in, or achievement of this purpose.

A major theme that emerged from our study is the way companies act on their awareness that encouraging a culture of ethics is an integral part of business today. Pilgrim's Pride is aware that its success and contributions are intertwined with the vitality of small communities throughout the United States. When communities benefit, Pilgrim's Pride benefits. Pilgrim's Pride is very careful to protect communities and natural resources in its use and operations on a day-to-day basis.

Striving to Achieve the Highest Level of Ethical Importance

NCR has had a longstanding commitment to "doing the right thing," stated William (Bill) Nuti, Chairman and CEO of NCR Corporation.

"Let's face it, a company can't survive for more than 124 years without paying attention to honesty and ethics in its business dealings. This attention to doing business the right way permeates NCR's culture. Actually, that is one of the primary reasons I joined NCR in 2005."

Nuti is clear about his expectations of integrity. "I can tell you that NCR's reputation is not something that is taken lightly by any of us in the company—in fact, it has been at the center of our daily work since the company was founded in 1884. As I convey regularly to our employees, our goal in business is to not only hit our plan, but to exceed it," he explained. "The same goes for striving to achieve the highest level of ethical performance. There is no room for error in the integrity of our reporting and our business. As a result, I expect each and every one at NCR to operate with the highest level of integrity.

"Along these lines, we want to make sure that we provide as much clarity as possible to assist employees in determining what is acceptable so they can incorporate these practices into their work at NCR," Nuti pointed out. "The company's Ethics & Compliance program is essentially grounded in that purpose. For example, the basic elements of the program are quickly and easily available to employees via the home page of the company's intranet site. NCR's Code of Conduct and corporate policies are available at that site as well for ready access to simplify the process and provide relevant information and guidance."

To encourage its employees and contractors—as well as customers, suppliers and other third parties—to report any potential wrongdoing or anything that they may see as questionable conduct, NCR established an "AlertLine" telephone number through which reports of potential wrongdoing or questionable behavior can be made. Callers can choose to report anonymously; however 50 to 55 percent of callers to the AlertLine choose to identify themselves.

To further assure callers of anonymity, Nuti specifies, the AlertLine is managed by a third party 365 days a year and—as NCR is a global company—is able to accommodate 75 languages.

The importance of clarity at NCR is borne out by its clear and robust Code of Conduct, an annual ethics and compliance training and certification module for employees and a variety of avenues for anonymously reporting questionable practices. The company's global reach stands out, with different languages spoken on its AlertLine.

More options are available to employees to contribute to protecting the company's reputation. They can also report questionable conduct to NCR's Ethics & Compliance Office, Law Department, or Corporate Security. "We want to ensure that all employees feel comfortable and secure in raising issues of concern in an effort to safeguard NCR's reputation," said Nuti. "One single incident can instantly destroy a company's reputation that has taken many years of compliant business and successful customer interactions to build. We have to do this, because if our company's reputation is not based on operating with the highest ethical standards, then we certainly don't deserve the trust of our employees and customers."

The companies in our study pay close attention to protecting reputational capital. Nuti, for example, underlines the importance of reputation and how quickly it can be lost even if it is carefully built up over the years. This awareness underlies the company's initiatives, such as the measures it takes to make employees feel secure and involved in safeguarding the company's reputation. "And let there be no misunderstanding," Nuti specified. "Anyone making a good faith complaint or reporting an irregularity is not subject to retaliation of any kind. This is something the company takes extremely seriously.

Any employee who retaliates against another employee for reporting such matters will face disciplinary action."

Nuti provided details: NCR conducts a Web-based Code of Conduct training and annual certification program in 13 languages, as well as other ethics and compliance training for all employees. Nuti reports that 100 percent of its employee base around the world was certified in 2008, commenting that this is a highly unusual and admirable benchmark for any global company. NCR also uses targeted training for specific positions within the company or particular countries. This targeted training covers subjects such as conflicts of interest, antitrust considerations, and anti-corruption laws around the world. Other initiatives, as well, contribute to a climate of ethics:

> To help keep ethics top-of-mind for employees, we regularly discuss during all-employee Webcasts real-life case histories of the types of ethical situations that one could encounter and also communicate at a high level what types of actions have been taken. This helps show that action does indeed result from employee participation in the process and reporting of any potential wrongdoing.

In addition, the Ethics & Compliance Office updates employees via quarterly email newsletters on disciplinary actions taken, including the number of terminations, suspensions, demotions and warnings for violations for NCR's Code of Conduct.

Here again we have the all-important mixed modes at work: the code, efforts to make employees comfortable in reporting questionable behavior, regular webcast discussions, the option to report to an auditor, and so on.

"Tone at the Top" Communication

Bringing ethics to the individual involves employees at all levels, as well as managers. Nuti's communication efforts work to ensure a culture of ethics. "I also believe it is vital for managers to 'set the tone' for their respective organizations as it relates to operating with integrity. One of the key elements that I assess is whether managers are setting the right tone and creating a culture of integrity, trust, and openness," he said, and continued: "With this in mind, I communicate directly to all of NCR's managers regarding my expectations about their leadership in this area. These 'Tone at the Top' communications, as I call them, set out in no-nonsense terms that, while we drive a performance culture in order to create a growth company, we will never compromise our Code of Conduct or our integrity in pursuit of profitably growing the top line."

To further solidify their efforts, NCR uses external assessments of their ethics and compliance programs to provide snapshots of how well their programs have been communicated and absorbed into their culture. The assessments also provide feedback on the areas in need of improvement. "As you can see, this is an area on which NCR places a high priority," said Nuti.

NCR is also guided by a set of "Shared Values." These are described by Nuti as "a consistent framework that directs our behavior, guides our decisions and helps us achieve our business objectives. At the very foundation of these Shared Values are the highest standards of integrity, including respect for each other, commitment to excellence, dedication to the customer, and accountability for success."

Nuti recalls ways in which employees have been involved. "When I joined the company, we undertook a company-wide initiative to gather employee input on how to make our Shared Values even stronger. We created a Web-based tool and discussion board on the company's intranet site where employees could provide their input and offer ideas on how to have each of the Shared Values further reflect those attributes considered important by employees," he noted. "We conducted global Webcasts and held discussion groups to ensure that employees had every opportunity to participate. We then analyzed the responses and communicated it to all employees, afterwards incorporating the refined Shared Values into the Code of Conduct training and certification as well as employees' performance objectives. Given the high-quality feedback from employees, this exercise only further solidified for me that NCR is a company truly grounded in 'doing the right thing.'"

Nuti's comments underline the importance of dialogue and the use of multiple modes to ensure employee involvement and help cultivate an ethical environment.

A Values-Based Approach Interwoven into Initiatives

Robert J. Stevens, CEO of Lockheed Martin, wrote to us about the company's "long-standing commitment to ethics, integrity, and 'doing the right thing.'" He explained, "Personally, I strongly believe that our ethical culture has been a key factor in the success of our corporation, and I fully support the ongoing ethics initiatives at Lockheed Martin. Our approach to ethics is values-based. We believe that ethical conduct requires more than simply complying with the laws, rules, and regulations governing our business. Ethics is first among our company values—the others are Excellence, 'Can Do,' Integrity, People, and Teamwork."

As Stevens describes the elements of Lockheed Martin's program and initiatives, his support is evident. His personal involvement exemplifies a key finding of our study: the relentless efforts by CEOs and companies to keep ethics at the top of people's minds throughout the organization.

We present the full list of initiatives that Stevens described. They represent an example of the myriad initiatives, intertwining written codes, training, helplines, ethics officers, and high impact ethics-related messages ... to name just a few. Especially interesting is the online availability of many materials produced by these initiatives. Lockheed Martin's Web site[4] represents a wealth of ethical archives open to multiple audiences.

Code of Conduct: Our Code of Ethics and Business Conduct, *Setting the Standard*, is published in 17 languages and distributed to employees around the world.

Chairman's Award for Ethics: Presented annually by me at our senior leadership meeting, this award goes to the Lockheed Martin employee who best exemplifies the corporation's commitment to ethics and integrity.

Ethics Awareness Training: Each year, all 130,000 Lockheed Martin employees are required to participate in one hour of live ethics awareness training. I kick off this effort with my direct reports, who then facilitate the training with their direct reports

---

[4]www.lockheedmartin.com

and so on, until the training has cascaded throughout the corporation.

Board Ethics Training: Each year I participate along with the other members of the Board of Directors in a discussion on ethics issues of relevance to the Board.

All-Hands Meetings: I have traveled to many of our company locations and spoken to thousands of employees on the importance of ethics and maintaining our ethical compass. One of these sessions was videotaped and included in our 2005 ethics awareness training introductory video.

Office of Ethics and Business Conduct: Headed by the vice president, ethics and business conduct, this position reports directly to me and to the Board of Directors. I meet regularly with the vice president, ethics and business conduct to discuss current issues and strategy.

Ethics and Business Conduct Steering Committee: Members include senior executives from each of the business areas and from key functional departments: legal, audit, human resources, communications, business development, finance, diversity, and ethics. The Committee oversees and provides strategic guidance to the office of ethics and business conduct.

Ethics HelpLine: A toll-free telephone number is available to all employees worldwide to seek guidance and to report concerns in the workplace.

Ethics Officers: We have full-time ethics officers at each of our major business units—part-time ethics officers at our smaller sites—who are available to offer guidance, respond to employee concerns, and coordinate investigations of employee wrongdoing.

Biennial Ethics Surveys: Every two years we survey our employees to gauge their perceptions on ethics, the application of our ethical principles, and satisfaction with their jobs and the corporation.

Compliance Training: We have developed 13 compliance training courses to ensure that employees are aware of the laws, rules, and policies applicable to their jobs.

Integrity Minute: A new initiative in 2005, these short video messages have an ethics theme and are sent to employees via e-mail.

Arts & Film Festival: Each year, employees are invited to use the creative arts to celebrate the shared culture of diversity, ethics, and leadership at Lockheed Martin. Participants may enter using any creative medium, including videos, photographs, poems, stories, posters, or animation. This must be done on their own time and using their own resources. The top entrants are recognized at an awards banquet. A "highlight reel" of the entries includes a congratulatory message from me to all participants.

Ethics Tools for Leaders: This training course is required of all members of management and provides leaders with the resources they need in maintaining a positive work environment and in responding to concerns raised by employees.

Ethics Tips for Leaders: These short ethics-related messages are sent to all leaders via e-mail. Two recent topics were building trust with employees and effectively facilitating ethics awareness training.

Ethics Communications: These include articles in company newsletters, posters, giveaways, calendars, and presentations to internal and external groups.

Ethics Orientation for New Employees: Within 30 days of hiring, each new employee is required to complete a course that includes the company philosophy on ethics, a decision-making model for handling ethics issues, an explanation on how the ethics process works when an ethics issue arises, and case scenarios covering common issues faced by employees.

These initiatives, along with Stevens's comments, show us that Lockheed has a complex web of self-reinforcing elements in place to support its ethical capital. The company has institutionalized practices that not only prepare employees for ethical attentiveness through training and specific demands, but also reward their ethical achievements. Lockheed is very specific and deliberate in its ethical practices. Certain initiatives allow it to take the temperature of the organizational climate, such as the survey, arts and film festival, and the all hands meeting. Yet other elements allow constant communication and serve as reminders of the value placed on ethics. The Integrity Minute, available online along with other materials, is one example.

This comprehensive system of practices helps Lockheed to secure employees' constant attention to ethics and helps them stay involved. It helps them recognize that ethical initiatives are not pro forma or point-in-time rituals but rather are actively pursued throughout the organization. And this involvement and attention to ethics, as our study shows, are all-important factors in building an honest corporation.

In the next chapter you'll see the other tools and channels CEOs and their companies are using to complement ethics-related initiatives such as the ones we've already presented.

Chapter 4

Making Ethics Messages Far-Reaching

WHAT OTHER TOOLS and channels are CEOs using to complement ethics-related initiatives such as the ones we discussed in Chapter 3? What other approaches are companies taking with their formal codes as part of their quest for ensuring ethical behavior? Clearly ethics efforts are not confined to a single moment or initiative. Mixed modes are constantly at work.

By taking advantage of a range of channels and formats to spread the word, CEOs make their ethics communication far-reaching. Personalized ethics messages can now be effectively conveyed via Web sites, DVDs, and CDs. CEOs have given speeches to groups outside the organization underlining the interconnection between business and society. CEOs have authored books, such as the one written with a former monk who had become the CEO's eyes and ears in building shared values. This chapter analyzes how CEOs and their companies enrich their ethical initiatives. It shows how messages may come in a variety of forms. CEOs use language strategically to keep integrity at the top of people's minds. These different styles and formats accommodate the differing preferences of individuals. They help to better internalize underlying values as well as what to do when faced with difficult choices. With materials and initiatives directed at multiple audiences, these efforts contribute to an ethical climate not only within but also beyond the organization. Even codes designed for employees have the potential to reach outside audiences because they are made available on corporate websites. Materials and codes are based on stable foundations, but they evolve over time according to changing contexts. These statements on initiatives, like those in Chapter 3, represent a snapshot in time that is worth examining.

Human Rights: The Changing Landscape, the Higher Road

Ethics is a global commonality. It affects industries and organizations everywhere. From time to time different areas come under scrutiny and debate, but at the core all companies are affected. This was the message delivered by William V. Hickey, President and CEO of Sealed Air Corporation, who spoke about ethics at the 2005 World Economic Forum in Davos, Switzerland.[1] He addressed the Forum on Human Rights and Corporate Social Responsibility with a

---

[1]We received the full text of Mr. Hickey's prepared remarks, which are longer than the speech actually delivered. He organized his remarks into four parts: (1) The Changing Landscape, (2) Sealed Air Corporation: The Higher Road, (3) Culture, and (4) The Road from Here.

discussion of issues connected to operating globally and having a multicultural workforce.

Hickey started by taking a broad view of corporate responsibility and human rights. "I think there are many indicators of a changing landscape on human rights. But one of them is surely the fact that someone representing a company like Sealed Air has been invited to participate on this panel."

The definition of human rights has expanded, as have the expectations placed on transnational corporations. Hickey commented on the evolution of what constitutes a human rights issue: "There was a time when discussions of corporate responsibility and human rights centered on the alleged political activities of fruit conglomerates in the jungles. More recently, we've seen textile and clothing companies move to the center of the debate. Now I think there is a growing sense that any corporation operating anywhere in the world is likely to encounter a human rights issue from time to time."

On the pervasiveness of human rights issues, he observed: "That's a by-product of globalization—more companies in more places. But it's also a result of an expanding definition of human rights. We've evolved from a definition bounded by political rights and physical security to one where economic and social rights and culture are part of the mix. And no matter where you are in the world, the workplace is always a nexus where economy and society come together."

Hickey said that the notion of corporate responsibility evolves as stakeholder groups grow. "As the parameters of human rights have been redefined, so have the expectations placed on transnational corporations," he noted. "We are currently engaged in a redefinition of corporate responsibility as so-called 'stakeholders'—a category sufficiently broad to include employees, regional neighbors, single-issue activist groups, and virtually anyone else who cares to stake a claim—seek growing influence on corporate decision-making.

"Add to this a growing number of groups organized to discourage bad corporate behavior...the United Nations' recently adopted norms to encourage *good* behavior," he commented, "and it becomes hard to imagine a future in which human rights are not a part of a corporate management portfolio."

Hickey observed that stakeholders have an increasing influence on corporate decision-making, which underlines the reciprocal nature of the relationship between corporations and stakeholders, and the need for greater transparency. But there is another implication: culturally diverse stakeholders make it harder to drive home key ethical messages. Corporations not only face dynamic environments, they simultaneously face a multitude of diverse employees and other stakeholders with varied objectives and different mindsets, who operate in different locations. This heightens the challenge of making their ethical messages and initiatives far-reaching.

Hickey then turned his attention to his own corporation: "I know some companies in other industries face tough human rights issues," he said. "I am grateful that I haven't had that kind of experience. There are certain types of knowledge I would just as soon do without. But from my vantage point at Sealed Air, I think two things are important in this regard."

Hickey's two key points derive from his own experience. "First, you must have clearly stated, written policies on what is right and wrong. And second, what you have in writing doesn't mean a thing if you don't have a corporate culture that *makes* it meaningful."

Hickey confirmed the all-important point that while clearly articulated codes are a must—for all countries, stakeholders, and borders—a shared culture that respects written ethics policies is also indispensable. The shared culture must value carrying out such codes, and they must be enacted by the employees. About Sealed Air's code, Hickey said: "Everyone who works at Sealed Air receives the company's written Code of Conduct. The code, for example, makes clear that we do not tolerate bribery, no matter what local custom or competitive pressures might encourage."

The Code points to the challenge of uniting and igniting the company's cultural momentum toward the same agenda (leaving aside, for example, the local custom that does not match the ethical imperative of the company). "At the end of the code, there is information about what to do if you see someone breaking the code, whether by treating another person disrespectfully or by engaging in unethical conduct," Hickey explained. "We contract with an outside service that operates our 'integrity hotline,' which employees or anyone else can call anytime directly or anonymously to report violations or abuse. They also receive my contact information and encouragement to contact me directly if there is a problem. I think that providing direct access to me underscores the importance we place on compliance."

How does Sealed Air face the larger issue of making ethical messages universal and far-reaching when different transnational locations come into play? Hickey replied: "From time to time, two different ways of doing business come into conflict. When that happens we opt for what we call the 'higher road.' So if our Code of Conduct is stricter, we apply the Code. If a local government regulation is more demanding, we follow the regulation. If it's a question of local cultural norms versus higher standards consistent with our corporate philosophy and practices, we choose our own way."

Importantly, Hickey addressed the potential for conflicting pressures on actions, specifying that at Sealed Air they take the stricter standard, "the higher road." Hickey's personal presence at the 2005 World Economic Forum and his communication of these codes demonstrated to his employees the importance of ethics and his pride in his company's ethical objectives and accomplishments.

Hickey considered the relationship between corporate culture and codes: "We need a written code of conduct so that all of us, working clear across the globe, are literally on the same page. But I'm sure the reason our people follow the code is not because it is printed in a handbook but because it is ingrained in our company culture," he observed. "Culture is much more influential than any document."

Hickey reinforces the value of a strong corporate culture: employees carry out what is indicated in the codes as a natural part of their work, not just because something is part of a handbook, however important written codes are. Hickey recognizes how multifaceted the culture is: "Our employees are accustomed to open lines of communication above and below, without a lot of formality or deference toward managers. We have worked hard to maintain a relatively flat hierarchy, so there are few layers of management and more individual autonomy."

Another important factor here is a structure that supports individual involvement in company policy and affords individual accountability. This openness characterizes relationships with other stakeholders, such as investors. "We've tried to maintain a similarly open posture toward capital markets and other external players," Hickey said. "After acquiring a large business unit a few years ago, we spent two years pursuing supermajority approval to eliminate a staggered board provision that came embedded in that unit's corporate structure. We tell our employees we 'trust in performance.' It's only right to tell investors the same thing."

Sealed Air's culture allows for individual autonomy and low formality. There is an open forum for communication across layers, levels, and departments. Sealed Air's trust in employee performance allows it to operate with less structure. More importantly, it allows each employee to feel they play an important role in carrying out the organization's objectives. "Our workforce is multicultural and international, but our way of doing business is not," Hickey continued. "We made a conscious decision to adopt a single model everywhere around the globe. That may conflict with some notions of cultural sensitivity, but we think it's consistent with fundamental values and rights. We believe it works both for our human relations and for our business."

By definition, a model like this may not always be in line with local customs. "There are certainly times when it runs counter to local custom," Hickey said. "In one of the countries where we operate, a woman who becomes engaged or pregnant is presumed to be tendering her resignation. We reject that. In fact, we have hired pregnant women in that country. But we also try to remain open to the many positive influences we encounter around the globe. Some of our best women engineers, for example, are found in eastern Europe.

"The bottom line is that our culture—our way of being internally, our way of treating one another, our way of looking at the world—ultimately determines how we behave toward others. Human rights are based on a recognition of human dignity. If you treat people with dignity, you shouldn't have human rights problems."

Sealed Air's care in employing a consistent approach to doing business—to "fundamental values and rights," even if it runs counter to local custom—is an important element in ensuring that its ethical stance remains steady across countries. Hickey underlines the importance of dialogue and the role of transnational corporations in human rights initiatives. "Looking ahead, I think the increase in corporate transparency will continue to yield human rights benefits. No transnational corporation wants to appear insensitive to human dignity," he explained. "And continued discussion and exposure—like this panel—will help move that along. But as long as there are gross disparities in the value placed on human life—and we all know those disparities exist—we will continue to have problems. Corporations can be part of the solution. But only a part. Human rights are still largely the province of governments, not businesses. The best corporations can do is clean up our own houses and set a positive example. It's not an end to the problem, but it's a start."

Hickey's message is indeed far-reaching: It is persuasive testimony that corporations, no matter where they operate, must take the lead and initiate corporate vigilance, rather than wait for regulations to materialize.

The President's Newsletter

We have underlined the way multiple modes used by the companies in our study work together to build a climate of ethics. The President's Newsletter[2] by William V. Hickey represents another example

---

[2]Sealed Air, President's Newsletter, November 8, 2004, no. 04–09.

of careful articulation of ethical efforts—in this case a new Code of Conduct. Like a team player, Hickey includes himself with employees, and stresses that "we all have a personal responsibility to know and follow the Code of Conduct, to report problems, and to ask questions when we are unsure." Highly effective CEOs see themselves on the same team as their employees. They share employees' goals. The newsletter is shown below:

Dear Fellow Employee:

Sealed Air has a reputation for conducting its business on a highly ethical level. It is important that we continue this record of integrity in the future. Our **Code of Conduct** is fundamental to our way of doing business and governs everything we do. As we pursue each of the Strategic Initiatives, it is important to remember that our reputation and continued success depend on our commitment to doing business with integrity and in full compliance with our Code of Conduct.

As it says on our #1 Card, our Code of Conduct is fully in effect...all the time...everywhere.

Earlier this year, our Board of Directors approved revisions to our Code of Conduct. The new Code of Conduct is posted on employee bulletin boards throughout the Company. Copies are available from your local Employee Development representative. We encourage you to read the new Code of Conduct. In the coming months, you will be asked to participate in training to further enhance your level of understanding of this vital part of our corporate culture. The training program will ensure that we all understand the important principles of the Code of Conduct, which are fundamental to help "Create a Performance Culture" in accordance with our high standards.

Remember, we all have a personal responsibility to know and follow the Code of Conduct, to report problems and to ask questions when we are unsure. We want to assure you that any time you feel that our integrity as a company is being threatened or compromised, you can speak freely about it without fear of retaliation. If you have any questions or concerns, you can discuss them with your supervisor or any other manager in the Company or with a member of the Law Department or the Employee Development Department.

We also understand that, sometimes, speaking face-to-face about your concerns may not be the most comfortable thing to do. For those times, we provide the Integrity Line, a 24-hour-a-day phone line that you can call to report any situation that could potentially violate our Code of Conduct or damage our Company's integrity and reputation.

One of the most important aspects about the Integrity Line is that, when you call, you may choose to remain anonymous. The Integrity Line is operated and staffed by another company, not Sealed Air. Instead of your name, your call will be assigned a code number and a randomly selected PIN. Your call will never be traced or recorded, and even if you do choose to give your name, you will not be retaliated against for making the call.

Additional information on how to deal with actions or circumstances that appear to be inconsistent with our Code of Conduct is attached to this Newsletter. The information explains how to contact the Integrity Line. We hope that you will never experience a violation of our Code of Conduct, but if you do, you should feel comfortable speaking with your supervisor, with another manager in the Company, including myself, or with the Integrity Line.

Each and every employee of the Company and its operations throughout the world is responsible for the maintenance of our fine reputation. We expect that each employee will support the Company's principles of business ethics and behave in a manner consistent with these high standards.

In this example, Sealed Air uses the newsletter, representing the voice of the CEO, as a vehicle to remind employees of the all-important fact that each employee is personally responsible for understanding and carrying out the Code of Conduct. Mixed modes are once again at work. Like other organizations intent on building a climate of ethics, Sealed Air holds training sessions to ensure consistent and profound interpretations of its Code of Conduct. It also offers opportunities for employees to report deviations. With sensitivity, it takes steps to ensure there will be no repercussions for employees who voice their concerns and promises to protect their identity if they wish to remain anonymous.

Sealed Air offers a choice of vehicles to report inconsistencies with its code, including phone, e-mail, Internet, and conventional mail. It also offers direct contact with the audit committee of the Board of Directors. A summary text outlining a range of alternative contact and referral options opens with the heading: "Concerns about actions or circumstances that appear inconsistent with our Code of Conduct should be dealt with as follows." In this case, effectiveness is increased by an easy-to-read format and a text that addresses the employee's concerns about feeling comfortable and making sure the matter is resolved.

Setting Both Direction and Values

"Several times a month," said Peter A. Darbee, President and Chief Executive Officer of PG&E, "I go out and meet with our employees to share our vision, strategies, and values with them. I expect, and frankly require, that other officers of the company do the same." He sent us a visual with a pyramid,[3] writing: "You can see that deeply embedded in this pyramid and, in fact, in the foundation, are our values. I believe it is the responsibility of the Chief Executive Officer to work with his/her leadership team to set both the direction and the values for a company."

The pyramid allows for a rippling effect throughout the organization. The tone and momentum is set and put forth at the top, but

---

[3]The pyramid is divided into levels, and each level answers questions appearing to the right of the pyramid and not shown above. For example, the top level about vision answers the question "why (our work is meaningful)," the second level down indicating "how we will know" answers the question "what (we will accomplish)," the third level down on "our strategies" answers the question "how (we drive our business)," and the next level, at the base of the pyramid, answers the question "how (we need to behave)."

everyone is responsible for keeping things in motion. At the same time, the base represents a stable foundation to be built up.

PG&E was presented in Chapter 2 in regard to the challenge of change. Darbee wrote to us about ethics initiatives, enclosed a video used for offsites, and also described how the pyramid outlines PG&E's vision, strategies, and values.

Darby said that the pyramid incorporates the work of the 16 top PG&E officers and reflects many months of work. We include the key points presented in the four levels of the pyramid, from the top level to the wider base. Although a list format cannot replicate the original's visual quality and impact, the content and statements show what is central. Peter Darbee's visual metaphor of the pyramid shows a domino effect. At the apex, questions of how, on what and why are answered from a base of ethical behavior.

Our vision:	The leading utility in the United States
How we will know:	Delighted Customers, Energized Employees, Rewarded Shareholders
Our strategies:	Operational Excellence Transformation
How we will work together:	We act with integrity and communicate honestly and openly

We are passionate about meeting our customers' needs and delivering for our shareholders

We are accountable for all of our own actions: these include safety, protecting the environment, and supporting our communities

> We work together as a team and are committed to excellence
> and innovation
>
> We respect each other and celebrate our diversity

The pyramid captures the essence of PG&E: Its personification, its mission, its vision, its way of operation, and its most important creeds.

Darbee gave us an example of how the company turns to their values as a moral compass when faced with a tough decision. "In connection with the Katrina disaster, the top team immediately reflected on our value of supporting our communities. We came together in agreement to make a contribution, not only on a corporate basis, but also on a personal basis," he noted. "That commitment was established immediately following the disaster, and checks went out the same week. Having set this leadership direction, we then turned to the employees of the company and requested they do the same. We believe that leadership is best demonstrated by doing rather than by talking."

CEOs make their messages far-reaching not only with words but with actions. They set examples that employees can follow. Most important, they create opportunities for positive action.

Energy and Action in an Ethical Agenda: Comments to Shareholders

Whatever the setting or context, we see a recurring theme: CEOs reinforce their understanding of their companies and the importance of ethics. In one example, at the FPL Group's 2003 annual meeting of shareholders, FPL chairman, president and CEO Lew Hay returned to the podium to comment on corporate governance matters.[4] He ensured that the energy and action in an ethical agenda came across loud and clear.

Hay began by addressing the shareholders and expressing pride in results—a natural way to start such remarks at an annual meeting of shareholders. "I hope you—our shareholders—will agree that all this adds up to a very strong company with excellent prospects going forward," he said. "I'm very proud of the fact that these accomplishments have been achieved in an environment that demands the utmost in integrity and accountability."

Taking advantage of the setting to communicate the company's stance on ethics, he continued, "So let me spend a few minutes talking with all of you about our views and actions in these areas, commonly discussed together under the umbrella terms 'corporate responsibility' or 'corporate governance.'"

Hay underlines the company's achievements in a demanding environment as a springboard to discuss integrity and accountability. "First, I want to assure you that no issue is of greater importance to our Board of Directors, our senior executive team and me personally than this one," he said, underlining his own personal involvement. "This company has long been a leader in corporate responsibility

---

[4]Excerpts from presentation by Lew Hay, Annual Meeting of Shareholders, FPL Group, May 23, 2003, Palm Beach Gardens, Fla., as prepared for delivery. Mr. Lew returned to the podium after he had already made initial remarks, followed by presentations of business results by several other executives.

and corporate governance activities. For example, some years ago we were one of 14 companies given an A+ rating in the first national survey of corporate responsibility policies conducted by the California Public Employees Retirement System.

"Today," Hay continues, "our corporate governance practices—which by the way are modeled after the very best practices in U.S. industry—are recognized by numerous organizations as being better than most in U.S. industry." The role of industry benchmarks in corporate governance stands out. There is no absolute checklist for ethics that allows a company to know when it is fulfilling its corporate responsibility.

"One organization—Institutional Shareholder Services—has determined that we rank in the top 20 percent of both our industry and the S&P 500," said Hay. "In fact, our rating would be even higher were it not for the fact that we're incorporated in Florida—which we have to be to maintain our status as an exempt utility holding company—and certain provisions of the Florida statutes are not deemed favorable to shareholders."

Hay lauded FPL for achieving such high ethical standing in an environment where such accolades are sparingly granted. He showcased FPL's attention to implementing many practices proactively, before new laws made them necessary. He provided examples: the active involvement of FPL's board in reviews and evaluations of performance, candid discussions among board members, the preponderance of independent directors, the session at every meeting where independent directors can meet without management members present, and regular benchmarking. These practices demonstrate how seriously the company conducts its corporate governance and how comfortable it is with transparency and interaction among its members. Hay's concise remarks below underline the energy and action behind FPL's ethical agenda:

- Hay showcased diversity and candidness. "We have an active and engaged Board of Directors. We have a good group of talented executives with a diversity of experiences and varying lengths of service," he noted. "The Board is very involved in understanding and approving business strategies—and in reviewing and evaluating the company's short- and long-term performance. I can assure you we have good candid discussions."

- Hay confirmed the independence of directors and lack of direct influence. "Today, all but two of our directors are independent of management," he stated. "Our compensation and audit committees have been comprised solely of independent directors for many years, as has our corporate governance committee since its inception in 2001."

- Hay affirmed that there is time to meet away from the full table, saying, "Additionally, the agenda for every regularly scheduled board meeting includes time for an executive session where the independent directors, if they so choose, can meet without management members present."

- Hay communicated the board's approach of always checking and "taking the temperature." He explained, "On a regular basis, the board and the board committees benchmark themselves against the best practices of other companies and adopt changes accordingly." Regular evaluations are part of this, and, he continued, "on an annual basis, the board evaluates its own performance."

- Hay highlighted proactive and innovative behavior. "As you know, over the past year there have been new laws passed and regulations approved for use in improving corporate governance," he said. "I believe you will find it reassuring to know that your board and your company were already in compliance with most of these mandates before they were required or even proposed."
- Hay underlined that the company strives to set the example and keep ahead: "I can assure you that despite the board's strong track record in this area, it continues to be committed to improving in this area and being among the best in our industry and among companies across all industries."
- Senior executives must support the front lines. "Beyond the Board, our senior executive team stays close to the day-to-day operations of our business," he continued. "We know where our revenues come from and how the company earns its money. We understand the risks the company is undertaking in the course of carrying out our business, and we have strong controls in place for managing those risks."
- Officers and managers are required to stay ethically literate. "A Code of Conduct for employees, which we're now updating, has been in place for many years," Hay said. "We require our top 200+ officers and managers to certify annually, in writing, their compliance with this code."

Hay's comments detail how FPL views its governance practices as an obligation to stakeholders and has adopted a process of continuous improvement as a way of ensuring success. "I want to add a very important point here," Hay stressed at the end of his speech. "We look at this issue of corporate governance in an increasingly broad and holistic way at FPL Group. Corporate governance is not just about compliance with federal law or New York Stock Exchange rules—as important as all that is. Nor is it just about having an independent Board—as important as that is. It's also about taking the right actions to sustain the company's success—satisfying customers and shareholders—over the long term."

The Role of Employees in Maintaining a Reputation for Excellence

At Computer Science Corp (CSC), one of the ways ethical practices and expectations are communicated is via video message to employees at their hiring, when communicating purpose is paramount. Quoting from their corporate facts:[5] "Our purpose is clear: Deliver innovative business and technology services that help our commercial and government customers achieve what they want most—Results."

The video message addresses how ethics issues may manifest themselves on a day-to-day basis at CSC and how employees can avoid them. This is another mixed mode at work: a story or anecdote is presented, followed by a description of the appropriate behavior or the answer to a question. The ethical principle is recalled at the end

---

[5]http://www.csc.com/about_us/.

of the example. CEO Michael Laphen delivered the opening and closing messages of the video in his previous role of Chief Operating Officer.

The narrator reminds viewers of CSC's commitment to excellence and ethical conduct: "The pursuit of technical excellence and the highest standards of professionalism are the hallmarks of Computer Science Corporation," he begins. "At CSC we are committed to ethical business practices in all our engagements around the world, and our employees' business conduct at all levels is vital to our continued success. We are known for our high standards and ethical conduct. This program will provide valuable information regarding the important role that each CSC employee plays in maintaining that excellent reputation."

A message delivered by Laphen, the CEO, then takes center stage. Laphen is careful to communicate that each employee contributes to CSC's ethical business practices: "Our company has always relied upon our dedication to ethical business conduct. We have earned the respect of clients and associates around the world for our professional integrity as well as for our technological expertise," he affirmed. "The consequences of violating the rules of ethical business practices are severe. It's your responsibility to know the rules and to follow the rules. Each of us is accountable for helping to maintain our sterling record of doing the right thing."

By giving specific attention to the company's code of ethics, he emphasizes the importance of the document and individual accountability. "To aid you in this task, we have published our code of ethics and standards of conduct, which is available in print and on the CSC portal," he explained. "This document contains valuable information on your responsibilities and accountability. Please read it carefully and if you have any questions at all, contact your manager or call human resources."

CSC communicates the far-reaching presence that it has as a business and the responsibility each employee has in maintaining what those before them have carefully built: "a sterling record of doing the right thing." The message makes it clear that there are consequences for not upholding CSC's ethical business practices. The next part of the video makes the connection between everyday activities and the decisions they require—decisions that have an impact on a company's ethical stance.

"Every day, new situations require thoughtful decisions," the narrator tells viewers. "Decisions could have a serious impact on the company and on the decision makers. The following are some examples of ethical issues you may encounter."

The first example, below, comes under the label of "internet plagiarism." CSC is very clear about which behaviors are acceptable and gives examples of possible ways that their ethical code might be violated. This approach helps employees acquire similar interpretations of its policies by addressing areas of breach. The title appearing on the screen is "Plagiarism and Copyright Infringement are Illegal."

The narrator poses a question: "If you were searching the internet for information that a client has asked for and you find articles written by someone outside of CSC, can you use these articles for your client's needs?"

He supplies the reply: "Yes, you can, provided you credit the source of the material. But representing someone else's work as CSC's or failing to attribute work to the author is contrary to CSC's standards."

To introduce the sections that follow, we have used the same titles shown on the screen to drive home a key message and introduce a discussion.

Avoid Situations that Suggest or Represent a Conflict of Interest

"Conflict of Interest" is another area addressed by the video. "Each CSC employee must be careful to avoid situations that might involve a conflict of interest or appear questionable to others. CSC has working relationships with many vendors around the world. Often in order to try and increase their level of business, vendors may send small promotional items to their contacts at CSC. Token marketing items are acceptable gifts. Expensive gifts are not. CSC employees with procurement related responsibilities may not accept anything of value from a supplier. Other CSC employees may accept modest gifts but nothing that might be considered excessive or intended to influence the employee's decisions."

Account for All Time on a Project

"Time Keeping" is another area addressed in the video. "All CSC employees are responsible for preparing all CSC business documents as completely, honestly, and accurately as possible. Regardless of the circumstances, you should report all of your hours worked on a project. If you were told to do otherwise, discuss your concerns with management or a human resources representative."

Unauthorized Copying and Sharing Licensed Software Can Create a Liability for CSC

Issues connected with Software Licensing are also addressed, with the narrator setting the scene for a possible dilemma: "CSC often licenses software from developers. Clients may want to obtain a copy of this software. What should you do if this occurs? It is permissible to arrange a demonstration of a software for the client; however, you should explain to the client that copies of the software may not be made unless CSC's license permits it as well as use by a third party. Our conduct on behalf of CSC with customers, suppliers, the public, and one another must reflect our high standards of honesty, integrity, and fairness."

Keep Proprietary Information Confidential

The video also addresses "Proprietary Information" with this scenario: "Each of us has an obligation to protect all CSC and customer data, property, and funds under our control against loss, theft, or misuse. It is possible that a friend or family member may ask you to provide them with some data that may help them win a position at CSC. This data could be several organizational charts or a list of current or potential new clients."

Here we have a specific example of a possible decision facing an employee. "What should you do?" asks the narrator. "In circumstances like this one," he explains, "direct the other person to the CSC website, which will provide him or her with an insight into CSC, its services, and some key clients. We must keep all proprietary information confidential and not make any of it available to any unauthorized personnel."

The narrator emphasizes that reports of suspected breaches remain confidential: "It is important to note that reporting a suspected impropriety will not be detrimental to a CSC employee. Reports will be treated in confidence consistent with the fair and rigorous enforcement of the CSC code of ethics and standards of conduct."

Michael Laphen's closing comments underlined the connection between success and high ethical standards, to be upheld by each individual employee: "The principals set forth in our code of ethics and standards of conduct reflect the type of behavior that has helped us earn the respect and success that we enjoy today with government and commercial clients around the world. Regardless of where we conduct business, we strictly adhere to the rules and laws of ethical practices of that country and of our own strict standards of professional business practices," he said. "I rely on each of you to adhere to these principles. As we strive for continued success remember that our foundation requires ethical conduct in our business relationships. CSC expects nothing less than the highest standards of ethical behavior from each and every one of you. Thank your hard work and dedication."

CSC makes it clear that they hope to uphold their reputation and ethical conduct as a source of worldwide respect and success. Laphen charges each employee with the important ethical responsibility of maintaining the code in their daily activities. "Each and every one" of CSC's employees is responsible for playing their role in achieving CSC's ethical agenda.

The Pro-Active Management of Culture as a Competitive Advantage

Doug Stotlar, CEO of Con-way Inc., presented a case study of what he likes to call "the pro-active management of culture as a competitive advantage." Con-way Inc. provides the full range of transportation and supply chain management services through its three primary subsidiaries: Con-way Freight, Con-way Truckload, and Menlo Worldwide Logistics.

Stotlar began with branding, saying, "When the leadership team identified four operating values it was decided that these values should have a 'brand look' so that various items could be used in this initiative such as hats, mugs, shirts, etc." Symbols representing four stars were adopted to create this look. In three of Con-way's business units, the Four Star logo represents the values of Safety, Integrity, Commitment, and Excellence.

"Con-way proudly displays this logo on numerous objects and in a variety of creative ways throughout the environment," said Stotlar. The logo, he noted, "symbolizes the collective commitment to the values that have made this organization strong and that will ensure future success." Each star was specially designed to support the value it represents.

The Gold Star—Safety: This star is first because Safety must be the number one concern of a transportation company. The design of this star is reminiscent of the stars worn on military or law enforcement uniforms. It was created to have an official, no-nonsense look. Safety is a no-nonsense issue at Con-way.

The Red Star—Integrity: The second star was designed to have a dimensional look because integrity is more than simply that one word. Integrity also means fairness, respect, compassion, courage and much more.

The Green Star—Commitment: The Commitment star is not fancy, it has no special design, it is not complicated. Its straightforward design is like the value it represents: When it comes to Commitment; it's either there or it's not.

The Orange Star—Excellence: This star symbolizes what has made Con-way the industry leader. Excellence in everything we do both internally and externally is the trademark of the organization. The design of this star reflects a similar design found in the corporate and component logos.

Con-way's efforts to portray its operating values visually and its enthusiasm for them are embodied in a logo that is displayed prominently throughout the organization. This form of visual stimulation serves as positive reinforcement, encouragement, and a testament to the widespread reach of its efforts. Logos are triggers that remind individuals of a broader mission. We can also note that Con-way's stars represent challenges inherent in their business—transportation—and highlight values that are most relevant to Con-way in their day-to-day business.

Pat Jannausch, Vice President of Culture for Con-way, tells how the initiative evolved when a new CEO was named in 2005. Doug Stotlar, formerly the CEO of Con-Way Transportation Services, determined that bringing improvements to the entire enterprise required a new organizational structure. This new structure would change Con-way from a holding company to an operating company, with a common approach to managing culture, a single vision, and a focused strategy for growth and continued success. Stotlar outlines the way the vision and the strategy were formally articulated at this stage of the process:

The Vision:

With the appointment of a Vice President of Culture, the CEO determined that the phrase and concept, *The Power of the Dream*, would symbolize the culture of the entire Con-way enterprise and that best practices from the business unit that first adopted this program would be shared with all business units. This concept would be further defined and supported by separate Constitutions created at the individual business unit level.

The Strategy:

A key element in each Constitution would be a logo where stars represent each of the core values, three of which will be common to all Con-way business units: Integrity, Commitment, and Excellence. The fourth star will represent an additional value that is core to each individual business unit based on its unique imperatives. For example, Con-way Freight's additional star is Safety. Menlo Worldwide Logistics chose Leadership.

To ensure a clear understanding of the role the core values play in culture and overall business strategy, each Constitution document will further describe the four values it espouses with three to five bullet points (norms) for each value. These points will explain what the individual value 'looks like' in daily behavior and decision-making in that business unit and will clearly state the expected habitual patterns in each case.

Within each business unit's Constitution, a Statement of Purpose or Mission will describe the nature of the business, what is important to it (values), the role values play in their business strategy and imperatives, and the pledge that organization makes to three key stakeholder groups: customers (internal and/or external), employees and shareholders.

The identification of the additional value (star) and its 'look,' clarification of expected behaviors (bullet points), and the Statement of Purpose/Mission will be developed by each individual business unit's leadership in facilitated sessions with the Vice President of Culture.

In this example we can see that Con-way is careful to specify, on a business-unit level, its expectations for the adaptation of each value in the various functions of its business. Like the companies highlighted in this chapter, Con-way pays attention to how values are enacted on a day-to-day basis and is careful to provide a clear platform upon which employees can understand overall corporate priorities.

Con-way keeps the culture of ethics alive through its Employee Recognition Program. The company has found this program essential as it upholds and fosters a culture of values-driven behavior by recognizing values-driven performance. The program consists of four levels of recognition and is notable in that employees can formally recognize fellow employees. Jannausch provided us with details about the levels:

1. Star Cards: These are small note-type cards with envelopes presented by anyone to anyone when outstanding values-driven behavior is exhibited.

2. Quarterly Leader Award: Through an online nomination process (paper forms are available as well), employees nominate one another for this recognition. A small number of employees—about 5 to 15, depending on the size of the company—are selected each quarter and presented with a small crystal statue.

3. President's Award: From the quarterly winners, the president of each business unit selects a small number of employees (again, about 5-15) who exhibited outstanding values leadership in that company. This selection takes place after the close of the fourth quarter. Soon after the start of the year, people join together for a celebration and presentation banquet event with spouses or special guests.

4. CEO Constellation Award: This is the highest level of achievement at Con-way. Recipients are chosen from the President's Award winners throughout the enterprise. A day of one-on-one interaction with the CEO is the key element in the winners' award package.

Jannausch provides details about a recent survey in which 395 Con-way employees were asked open-ended questions about what three things in their company's culture most contribute to their commitment to the organization. The response rate was high, with 352 responses and a good 106 of those about values. Here's a sampling of employee comments which underline their awareness of values.

- Safety, Integrity, and Commitment to Excellence
- The core values, especially commitment, excellence, and integrity keep me committed to Con-way

- The core values they have set forth
- The "power of the dream"
- Our core values stand for the type of person I am proud to be
- Values-based management
- Our values are my push every day
- Integrity—this value is deeply embedded in our culture
- The four stars and the values they represent
- The expectation of continued Excellence, Integrity, and Commitment to Safety
- Our commitment to our core values
- The company's commitment to the Mission Statement
- That our documented values are more than just printed words on a banner. They truly guide behavior and are a part of our cultural fabric
- My department head lives our core values
- That our mission and values are non-negotiable
- Follow our core values and all will work out

Since the start of the initiative in 1999, Con-way employees and managers around the globe have come to realize the value and importance of managing their culture. Con-way's culture affects its ability to recruit, engage, and retain employees. It supports the productivity and teamwork needed to prosper in an extremely competitive industry. Below is a list of some additional ways through which Con-way manages culture:

- Recruiting—Values driven communication regarding the nature of the company

- Employee orientation—Culture orientation as a foundation module
- All training programs as appropriate—e.g., Leadership and management development, coaching, effective communication, etc.
- Environment—Poster, banners, etc.
- Coaching and Discipline—Discussion of relevant values and violations
- All communication from leaders—Written and verbal to reflect values and mission in appropriate ways to the extent possible
- Management meeting agendas—Culture is always a topic
- Annual enterprise celebration—*Keeping the Dream Alive*
- Annual Values Task Force Chair meetings—To share best practices
- Annual "Eagle Meeting"—Leadership opportunity to discuss culture management

In 2003, Con-way celebrated its twentieth anniversary with the Stars and the Constitution playing a key role in the celebration. In 2004, the fifth anniversary of *The Power of the Dream* was acknowledged with a special *Keeping the Dream Alive* celebration. And in 2008, Con-way will be acknowledged for 25 years of industry leadership with their Stars at the heart of their celebration.

Specificity and Meticulousness

Michael Coppola, President and CEO of Advance Auto Parts, gave us a closer look at how that company takes great care to ensure profound understanding and meticulous implementation of its Code of Ethics and Business Conduct. For them, specificity is a key element.

Advance Auto Parts' Team Member Handbook outlines the company's Code of Ethics & Business Conduct, which Advance expects every Team Member and vendor to abide by. One element of this code that is referred to regularly pertains to gifts. Advance strictly outlines appropriate conduct, even for "routine" business functions, in order to avoid conflicts of interest. For example, the policy calls for Advance to purchase business meals when vendors visit Advance's offices, and for vendors to purchase business meals when Advance visits their offices. The policy recommends at least two Advance Team Members attend all business dinners, "in order to avoid a single individual being wined and dined (or worse yet, bribed) by a vendor."

This policy also governs the acceptance of gifts, which are limited to "infrequent gifts valued at less than $50, as long as the Team Member's supervisor is made aware of the gift." Gifts of larger value should be declined and reported to the Team Member's supervisor. "In one recent case," Coppola recounted, "a Team Member received a gift from a vendor genuinely given in recognition of her wedding. The gift, however, was valued at approximately $100, and our Team Member returned the gift—paying the postage for return-shipping out of her own pocket."

Stories, we found, serve ethics on multiple fronts. Advance Auto Parts strengthens adherence to the Code by supplementing it with stories about employees and their level of commitment to compliance.

Coppola also cited one of Advance's former Board members (Stephen Peck, who died tragically in 2004), who had a saying about corporate integrity that has stuck with Advance: "To be appropriate, our actions must not only be right, but also look right."

Coppola explained with examples specific to Advance's business activity. "In other words, the mere perception that an activity is unethical makes it inappropriate, even if the activity itself is acceptable," he said. "What is the perception if a sales clerk at an Advance store rings up his/her own purchase? If rung properly, the transaction would 'be right,' " he explained. He elaborated on the scene, saying, "What if the sales clerk discounted the merchandise? Again, this could be entirely appropriate (if the sales clerk applied his or her customary Team Member discount). But because this could be perceived inappropriately," he explained, "Team Members should have their personal purchases rung by another cashier."

Advance, then, offers employees an important tool for assessing the appropriateness of actions: What will someone else think of this action? Even if it is appropriate, could it be perceived as inappropriate? This is an important benchmark to offer employees when they are trying to balance business with ethics. Complex situations don't always match the written codes. Thus such a question about perceptions can help align personal values with ethical initiatives.

Advance also created a supplemental Code of Ethics for Finance Professionals. Coppola explains that this was done in response to the well-documented accounting scandals at Enron, WorldCom, and other companies in the late 1990s and early part of the following decade. This document is circulated annually to the company's accounting, financial reporting, investor relations, tax, and treasury professionals, who are required to sign the document as an acknowledgement that they recognize and accept their responsibilities. This Code of Ethics not only delineates acceptable versus unacceptable conduct, but also requires the company's finance professionals to report any known or suspected violations of the code.

In other words, failing to report others who are violating the code is itself a violation of the code. The company provides a confidential toll-free hotline, through which Team Members can report violations anonymously. The hotline is staffed by a third party, which passes along any reported violations to the company's Human Resources department.

Like other companies, Advance supplements its Code with a hotline. Importantly, Advance recognizes that different specialties within a company will call into question different ethical challenges, so they offer each a separate specific Code.

In late 2001, Advance Auto Parts became a publicly traded company, with its shares listed on the New York Stock Exchange. Having operated 70 years as a privately run company, Advance became subject to a host of new rules, regulations, and responsibilities as a public company. One outcome was the establishment of Advance's Regulation Fair Disclosure (Reg FD) policy. This policy outlines appropriate and inappropriate methods of communicating with the company's investors, including when and how these conversations can take place, what subject matters are off-limits, and which individuals within Advance are authorized to speak to the investment community. Of particular note, the policy requires authorized spokespersons to document each and every conversation with investors. They must detail the date of each conversation, who participated in the conversation, and the topics discussed. The policy also sets an expectation that at least two company spokespersons participate in conversations with investors, in order to ensure sensitive topics are kept off-limits. Following every conversation with a member of the investment community (whether by phone or in person), each Advance participant signs a form attesting to the fact that no material, non-public information was divulged. In so doing, the company has a living archive that it can tap into, should there be any inquiries about recent conversations with investors.

Again, Advance's meticulousness stands out. Advance takes great care in documenting all interactions to ensure a high level of ethical awareness.

In a similar vein, the company also has an Insider Trading policy, which governs the ability of Team Members to buy or sell company stock. This policy outlines the appropriate periods during which such transactions may or may not take place, and also discusses Team Members' responsibilities in terms of protecting confidential infor-mation—that is, not to share it with anyone outside the company (be it an investor, a competitor, a vendor, a neighbor, or family member). Senior officers of the company must "pre-clear" all trad-ing in the company's stock through Advance's General Counsel, who will either approve or deny the officer's request to trade, based on the time of year (whether early or late in a fiscal reporting period), whether the company possesses material inside information (about financial performance, potential acquisitions or divestitures, capital structure changes, etc.), and other factors.

"A reasonable question might be: Why does Advance care so deeply about honesty and integrity in the cutthroat world of busi-ness? The question almost answers itself," Coppola noted. "Integrity is good business in and of itself, precisely because the business world is so competitive. For example, Advance's Reg FD policy names five company spokespersons. No other individuals within the company are authorized to speak to investors or the media, unless authorized to do so by one of the five spokespersons. What does this accomplish? It keeps store Team Members and regional field personnel from inadvertently answering media questions that could provide valuable insight to our competition—about the location of a future store, for example."

These comments underline that Advance is very sensitive to a diverse range of ethical issues: from ensuring understanding and adherence to its Codes, to creating Codes for specific areas such as Finance, from helping employees make ethical and appropriate choices, and to specifying policies for employees trading company stock.

Sending Messages through Inspirational Statements

CEOs' words, tone, and thoughts have far-reaching influence. In examining the variety of materials and messages we received, their short and simple statements about what is actually complex stand out for emphasis and inspiration. Here are some examples from Curt S. Culver, CEO of MGIC Investment Corporation.

He sent notes and documents,[6] and he explained that they detail his request of MGIC coworkers to make a difference: to be a leader, take ownership, enjoy your life and work. This is something Culver addresses every year with coworkers at the State of the Company meeting.

---

[6]Mr. Culver's comments on ethics and the business community appear in Chapter 6.

The simplicity of his words—simplicity with impact—and the personal quality of his thoughts can really give the individual a sense of energy and the sense that "I can make a difference even by changing a single thought about how I approach a task." This kind of presentation allows one to interpret a thought in a meaningful way.

Be a Leader

It's not about title, but about talent and action. It's not about power, but about purpose. Because when you are a leader, you discover the purpose of life is to live a life of purpose. And to accomplish that, you need to live life with passion. You need to work with a passion. People love doing business with someone who loves their work.

Leaders never stop learning. Those who learn the most in this world will win. Knowledge is the key, so become massively competent. Through knowledge, you will control your career. (And your career won't be managing you.)

Take Ownership

Do the right thing. Leaders care more about doing the right thing than appearing intelligent. Take responsibility for your actions. Welcome failure—the highway to success. (Share the credit—take the blame.) Have strong principles. Principles are to people what roots are to trees. People who feel superb about themselves generate superb results—high self-esteem. Never settle on mediocrity when you can attain mastery.

Enjoy Your Work and Life

Your Work: Work should be fun. Control it—don't let it control you.

Work-Life Balance: [Balance] work, play, family, religion, charitable giving, and community work.

Good Humor: Laugh at yourself. Don't take yourself too seriously—take your job seriously.

Your Health: If you don't take the time for exercise now, you'll take the time for illness later.

Honesty: [Embody] personal and corporate honesty.

Hustle: If you don't like the results you are getting, you'd better change what you are doing.

Humility: Humility is the ability to begin something that doesn't end with you. As the saying goes, the first 50 years of your life are about building one's legitimacy while the last 50 are devoted to building one's legacy. And building a legacy is not about titles, wealth, or impressing others. It's not about reaching the top or looking good. Rather, it's about doing good.

In closing, Culver shared a quote by Leo Rosten: "I cannot believe that the sole purpose of life is to be happy. Rather, I think the purpose of life is to be useful, to be responsible, to be compassionate. It is, above all, to matter: to count, to stand for something, to have made some difference that you had lived at all."

"Make a difference with your life," stated Culver, "and I guarantee you will make a difference with your work."

Culver's inspirational statements underline the importance of balance and harmony in one's personal and professional life.

Codes of Conduct in Changing Corporate Culture

Any kind of change is a challenge. "Addressing and attempting to change a corporate culture is a long term effort that requires intense focus," said James T. Hackett, CEO of Anadarko Petroleum Corporation. "The task is made a bit simpler when the corporation is facing another major change—a crisis, new strategy, or changed leadership."

In the case of Anadarko, a change in leadership and strategy occurred in late 2003 and early 2004, but according to Hackett the company already had a strong ethical culture. He described the process of articulating corporate values and the role of written codes in changing corporate culture. "To reinforce this culture, the new team's first task was to codify our corporate values, of which the first value is to *act with integrity*," he said. "It doesn't get simpler than this. Management reiterates this value through a wide range of visible actions and communications, including conducting the company's first employee surveys to give employees a much needed voice in influencing the company's direction and policies."

Hackett provides some examples: "Employee town halls, monthly employee meetings, and other communication tools provide an opportunity for leadership to discuss the role ethics plays in business decision-making."

The company intertwined its articulation of formal codes with other initiatives that allowed dialogue and input from employees. This is a key part of building ethical organizations, as our study has shown. "The company established the Anadarko Code of Business Conduct and Ethics," Hackett said, "which promotes the following six objectives: honest and ethical conduct; avoidance of conflicts of interest; full, fair, accurate, timely and transparent disclosure; compliance with the applicable government and self-regulatory organization laws, rules and regulations; prompt internal reporting of code violations; and accountability. To reinforce the importance of acting within this code, the company hosts an anonymous telephone hotline that allows employees to report any apparent wrongdoing."

Hackett pointed out that these are "just a few examples of how Anadarko is making ethics an integral part of our employees' work experience." Stressing that words and actions must work together, he continued, "It's not enough to put it on paper—employees need to have tangible examples of decisions that reinforce integrity in action."

By bringing codes home to employees, companies contribute to a climate of ethics. By creating opportunities for dialogue among employees, Anadarko reinforces corporate values. The value of examples is clear, with the company initiating the momentum, providing a platform to build on, and using actions to teach by example. With such an approach, codes are not passive.

A Shared Moral Foundation for Business

Managing and staying ethically alert is a finely-tuned balancing act, but the benefits are far-reaching in terms of financial and ethical success. Written codes and standards guiding behavior help to ensure continuity as companies' operations expand over time. A document created four decades ago promulgates the cornerstone of ExxonMobil

Corporation's ethics policy: It is the company's *Standards of Business Conduct*, a text provided annually to every employee.

"Exxon Mobil Corporation is committed to managing its business in accordance with the highest standards of ethical conduct and corporate citizenship," said Rex W. Tillerson, its chairman and CEO. "Today, more than a century after its founding and with operations in more than 200 countries and territories," he said, "our company remains steadfast in adhering to a strong code of ethical and legal standards that guides our global enterprise."

Tillerson's words underline the importance of an ethical base for the company as well as its importance for a competitive market. "At ExxonMobil, we believe that our commitment to ethical behavior and honesty is not only the best business policy, but the only one compatible with free and competitive markets," he said. "History shows that no free society or competitive market can long prosper without a strong ethical base. It is only through a shared moral foundation—a set of binding rules governing what we understand to be ethical conduct—that voluntary commercial activity can flourish. Put another way, a sound business code of ethics is essential to the preservation of free enterprise."

ExxonMobil's long-standing support for the rule of law is absolute, Tillerson specified. "But our Ethics Policy does not stop there. Even where the law is permissive, the Corporation chooses the course of highest integrity. Local customs, traditions, and mores differ from place to place, and this must be recognized," he commented. "But honesty is not subject to criticism in any culture. In many of the new areas where our company is pursuing oil and gas development, the host country's legal system is under development or in transition. In these countries, we work with the host governments and nongovernmental organizations to create a legal and regulatory framework conducive to investment—a framework based on the rule of law.

"All of us in management know that we must continue to do many things well to remain a successful global enterprise over the longer term. We understand our responsibility to create sustainable shareholder value, continuously improve our operations, and provide a wide range of quality products to our customers," he affirmed. "We fulfill that responsibility by operating successfully in the interests of our shareholders, customers, employees, and society in general."

Often ethical challenges are embedded in the environment and have broader implications for the organization and for wider society. In the next chapter, CEOs will describe how their organizations approach ethical issues inherent to their industry.

Chapter 5

Being Ethically Alert to the External Environment

SOME ETHICAL CHALLENGES are inherent to particular industries. For some companies, ethical challenges surface in areas related to customer service. For others, ethical challenges lie in resource procurement or manufacturing processes. To foster a climate of ethics, the CEOs in our study are alert to the external environment and ensure that the business organization functions optimally. In an ethically aware culture, each individual brings the organization to its full potential while acknowledging that the organization is part of a larger environment to which it is accountable. In other words, stakeholders will define its success. Companies are proactive in building a culture that allows for innovation. For these companies, ethics encompasses a responsibility to the larger environment and is an integral part of the way they do business.

This chapter shows how some of the companies in our study approach ethical issues specific to their industries, and how they take advantage of these issues to encourage ethical behavior that is good for stakeholder groups and good for business.

Environmental Stewardship

"Maintaining an ethical business environment has been a top priority for TI since its founding," said Rich Templeton, CEO of Texas Instruments (TI). "We are committed to providing our employees with an inclusive, diverse workplace, to serving as an active and responsible part of our community, and to dealing fairly and honestly with everyone with whom we do business. Our products have changed through the years, but one thing that has remained constant is our values, and we're proud that throughout our history, we have maintained a passion for innovation and for making a positive difference in the world, both as a technology company and as a corporate citizen."

We have seen many examples of how a solid foundation of values serves companies well. This is also the case for TI. Like other companies in our study, TI stresses the need to go beyond compliance. "One area we consider critical to our success is environmental stewardship," Templeton explained. "A lot of companies say this, and most include 'compliance with environmental regulations' as part of their ethical code.

"The hard question that companies wrestle with, though, is whether or not just obeying the law is the ethical standard by which they want to operate," Templeton observed. "When it comes to ethics, what is the best approach for the business, the employees, the customers, and the community? Meeting minimum requirements or striving for something more ambitious? At TI, we asked ourselves this question early in our history and decided that ethical standards come from within, and that doing the right thing often means exceeding legal requirements and tackling environmental issues that haven't yet entered the public debate."

Templeton described TI's approach this way: "Rather than stopping at compliance, we rely upon our own values, as well as our skills as scientists and engineers, to minimize the environmental impact of our operations and to protect our employees and our communities to the best of our abilities."

Templeton addresses a very real dilemma: Should companies strive to meet the legal requirements or *exceed* them? Meeting minimal ethical standards doesn't form a bond among organization members. It doesn't invigorate them and motivate them to feel proud and leave behind a legacy built on their ethical efforts. Compliance itself is not motivating. The choice to exceed and be an example is a motivator. It motivates employees each day to make a difference on the ethical landscape.

Templeton's comments underline TI's proactive approach toward ethics and the environment: the company cultivates an identity connected to doing "the right thing." For TI, that means doing more than what is legally required. They must tackle issues that haven't yet entered the public debate. In this example, the company acknowledges regulations as platforms but ultimately takes responsibility for expanding on that platform. TI takes an evolutionary approach to ethics, addressing current and past issues, anticipating future issues, and connecting this to business performance.

"Setting high environmental standards is critical to employee morale and community relations, but it also supports our goals for financial performance. As a publicly held company, we have a responsibility to deliver earnings growth to our shareholders," Templeton noted, "and we have found that the more we demand of ourselves, with regard to the environment, the greater value we are able to bring to the business. Contrary to conventional wisdom that strong environmental stewardship increases costs, we've discovered that minimizing waste, safety hazards, and energy use helps increase our bottom line."

An ethical approach means not only doing the right thing, it also means making sound business decisions, which ultimately provide more value to shareholders. The company, employees, shareholders, and members of the community benefit. Templeton detailed TI's efforts. "In the 1990s, for example, we made environmental stewardship, along with workplace safety, a key initiative in our efforts to lower our manufacturing costs," he said. "As a result, in a single year, environmental, health, and safety improvements alone accounted for significant savings per chip.

"We then set more ambitious targets, and this was at a time when the semiconductor market had taken a dip, and our plants were underutilized," he continued. "Despite the challenging business climate, we succeeded in meeting our savings goal while delivering even greater environmental improvements."

What stands out is the way TI considers its approach to ethics and the environment an investment for the future versus a cost for the short term. The company goes beyond a simple form of stewardship, investing in building an ethically aware culture which anticipates and embraces—rather than reacts to—environmental and ethical challenges. TI's view of ethics as an integral part of business is evident in Templeton's description of TI's proactive approach.

"Another TI effort that has delivered real bottom-line value has been our commitment to getting ahead of environmental regulations," Templeton said. "Regulatory compliance has always been a priority, but we have found that being reactive in a rapidly changing global marketplace hurts our cost position."

Templeton states that being reactive would mean not being able to meet customers' "green" needs quickly enough. To meet them, "we take a proactive approach and anticipate legislation coming down the road," he said. "This enables us to prepare well in advance for future regulations and help our customers make necessary transitions. One example is TI's conversion to lead-free products, which is aggressive and well underway." TI stopped the use of lead in its products well in advance of legislation that mandated its removal.

Templeton provides background on this particular initiative. "We began the effort in the late 1980s when we announced one of the world's first lead-free semiconductor component finishes. This was long before the EU's adoption of its 2003 Restriction on Use of Hazardous Substances in Electrical and Electronic Equipment (RoHS), and also ahead of most of our competitors," he explained, "We then went on to convert all TI products impacted by RoHS to lead-free solutions prior to the restrictions becoming effective in July 2006. By addressing the issue early, we have been able to work with customers to develop effective alternatives and avoid costs down the road."

This example shows TI's ethically sensitive culture to be a priceless resource. By addressing issues early, the company is able to implement appropriate measures quickly and naturally—a stark contrast to the potential scenarios at organizations that have not built ethics and environmental awareness into their culture. Such companies are destined only to react to industry challenges, letting a crisis, legislation, or corporate community trend drive their decision. Being ethically aware is not only good for the environment and the community, it's also good for the company and its customers. The awareness builds preemption into their culture. TI builds on the business benefits of a culture of ethics.

"Because we've seen the positive results environmentally sound measures bring to our business, we've designed our newest facility in Richardson, Texas with the goal of reducing both environmental impact and operating costs," said Templeton. "We collaborated on the construction project with the Rocky Mountain Institute in an effort to create the world's first 'green' semiconductor manufacturing facility. Not only are our engineering teams delivering a 'green' facility for 30 percent less per square foot than the cost of the last conventional chip plant TI built, the Richardson site will deliver enough in annual savings to pay for the additional cost of the 'green' features within a couple of years of operation."

It is worth considering how the company's visionary approach came into being. "Over the last two decades, we've developed a vision for our environmental efforts that encompasses both our desire to do the right thing and our financial obligations to our shareholders." Templeton continued, "We believe our efforts to 'design for the environment' must go beyond eliminating waste. They must begin earlier in the process to anticipate and eliminate problems before they occur. In fact, we want to get to a point at which all our engineers, as they develop new manufacturing processes or product technologies, consider environmental concerns equally with all other factors. We believe that balance produces the right solutions for our employees and our communities and, in the end, the most cost-effective solutions as well."

Our study has underlined the progressive nature of ethics in these companies: honest organizations do not take a static approach to ethics. In the case of TI, the company tries constantly to minimize its environmental impact, increase its social contributions, and address issues before they emerge. In this manner, it helps its customers and makes attention to ethics a driving force in doing business in their industry. TI's approach is to constantly exceed previous targets. Their values are embodied in how they approach their business on a day-to-day basis—by innovating and considering the environment.

Such an approach, which gives attention to manufacturing processes and technology, is an important part of being an ethically aware company. This benefits employees, customers, and communities. The CEOs in our study and their companies redefine what it means to do the right thing so that it takes on greater significance. Enhanced ethical awareness is a fundamental part of doing business, as we have underlined throughout this book. Companies strive to "go beyond"—beyond compliance, beyond reacting, beyond what in the past was considered good enough to be a good corporate citizen or to be environmentally aware. Honest companies anticipate, preempt and meet the challenge well prepared.

Employing Honorable Business Practices

Pilgrim's Pride faces challenges of resource acquisition and resource development: raising and preparing their chickens for sale. Its animal welfare policy is an important part of their corporate identity. On a daily basis the company must ensure humane treatment of animals, and it must pursue its corporate mission as it employs the honorable business practices that make them proud. Although Pilgrim's Pride's challenge may at first seem unique because it is responsible for live animals, all companies ultimately affect lives. It is important to take a lesson from the delicate nature of Pilgrim's Pride's business.

Pilgrim's Pride Animal Welfare Policy[1]

Policy Statement

Pilgrim's Pride Corporation will strictly maintain a program of animal welfare that is designed to eliminate unnecessary harm and suffering for animals in the day-to-day operation of our production processes.

Implementation

Pilgrim's Pride has implemented live production practices that avoid unnecessary suffering, prevent destructive behavior, prevent disease, and provide proper nutrition for poultry while promoting good animal health.

Pilgrim's Pride has developed specific programs in cooperation with our customers which promote generally accepted standards for the welfare and humane treatment of the animals in our charge. These programs include both internal and external audit procedures.

Pilgrim's Pride also supports and has implemented the guidelines for animal welfare issued by the National Chicken Council and National Turkey Federation with the intent to promote the humane treatment and well-being of poultry through the production process.

Pilgrim's Pride has a documented training program for all Partners involved in handling live animals. All Partners involved

---

[1]http://www.pilgrimspride.com/aboutus/animalwelfare.aspx.

in handling live birds receive training in the areas that are appropriate for them in order that they can perform their jobs in accordance with best practices.

Employees or growers who violate the Pilgrim's Pride animal welfare policy and associated procedures will be subject to disciplinary action, up to and including termination of employment or termination of their grower contract.

Pilgrim's Pride's challenges are quite unique in that they involve live resources: chickens. Yet, the company recognizes that its business practices have much larger implications for the business environment. Its Animal Welfare Policy illuminates and operationalizes Pilgrim's Pride's ethical foundation. This has symbolic value to other organizations both within and outside its primary industry.

Culture and Creative Technical Tension

James T. Hackett, CEO of Anadarko Petroleum Corporation, explains how the reporting of oil and natural gas reserves, a technical aspect of the industry, is connected to ethics. This is a clear example of an industry-specific issue. Although in this case the industry challenge is steeper in that Anadarko cannot "see or touch" its product, their challenge speaks to the greater issue of self-reporting, with investors and the SEC involved.

"The exploration and production (E&P) industry basically performs two services," Hackett said. "Utilizing the sciences of geophysics and geology, we first explore for and ultimately identify hydrocarbons—oil and natural gas—in underground reservoirs. We then utilize engineering to move, or produce, the oil and natural gas from its reservoir to the surface of the earth.

"A company's reserves are defined as identified hydrocarbons that have not yet been produced," Hackett explained. "Oil and natural gas reserves, our company's most valuable asset, are under the ground, and each company is responsible for estimating their reserves' size and commerciality for investors and the SEC.

"In simple terms, we estimate how much oil and gas is down there, and how likely we'll be able to get it out," Hackett explains. "We then monitor and adjust that initial estimate over the life of the reservoir. It's a difficult science since we can't see or touch our product," he observed. "At year-end 2004, Anadarko had 2.37 billion barrels of oil equivalent of proved reserves worldwide."

Recent reserve write-downs by major energy companies have brought more scrutiny to the technical process of how companies account for their reserves. "New technology used both below and above the ground gives us more accurate data and improves our estimating capabilities," Hackett explains. "The science and reservoir engineering disciplines continuously develop new tools and theories that advance the process as well." Here, again, we can see the evolutionary nature of ethics. As new tools are made available for specific industrial needs, so changes the ethical terrain, but the importance of integrity remains constant.

But technical tools and theories are not all that goes in to estimating reserves, Hackett said: "I would argue that the company's culture contributes equally to the process, which must be based on both our capability and our integrity. The right corporate culture should lead the technical process and ensure an effective system to challenge reserve assessments.

"One term we use for this 'challenge' process at Anadarko is 'creative technical tension,' and the name implies the purpose it serves," he continued. " 'Technical tension' assures that you have set up an effective system of checks and balances as a component of that challenge mechanism. The concept goes further to ensure a direct interaction and exchange of ideas in the checks and balance process. Technical tension tries to achieve conflict without destructive dialogue and repercussions."

Hackett's comments underline the delicate nature of an issue inherent to his industry—the estimation of oil reserves and oil extraction—and its interconnection with Anadarko's culture. Anadarko communicates how serious it is about honesty in its estimation process and the importance it ascribes to the balance between technical tools and culture. Rather than a limited focus based on "more is better," Anadarko creates a challenge around the delicate estimation process that is a critical part of its business.

Anadarko creates "technical tension" through a number of methods. "The company's reserves review team—a group of employees along with an outside auditor—continuously reviews Anadarko's booked reserves," said Hackett. He also specified that employees on this technical team are intentionally removed from the company's financial bonus structure which, in part, rewards employees for meeting annual reserves goals. "The theory is that those who account for reserve estimation should have no financial gain in tallying the numbers," he noted. "Their purpose is to question, challenge, and audit our reserves estimation process, and we have created an environment that allows them to do that freely."

We can see that Anadarko is careful to build the right work environment to nurture a climate of ethics. This climate is fundamental to the business. The company is also careful to align values with reward systems. Anadarko's procedures help ensure honesty. They do not reward overestimation.

Anadarko also actively seeks feedback from employees. Encouraging dialogue, we've seen, is an important part of building a culture of ethics. "Our process also utilizes a questionnaire that we send to our technical staff about our reserves reporting process," said Hackett. "We ask open-ended questions and receive frank comments in return, some of which can be in contrast to supervisors' comments. This exercise provides us with valuable information not only on our reserves but on the internal process itself. Where are the discrepancies, and is there a pattern we need to explore? Creating open communication fuels the right culture and tells employees that they are empowered to act ethically in their daily decision making."

Anadarko uses various modes to build a culture of ethics. It encourages dialogue and also uses a system of checks and balances to ensure honesty in every aspect of its estimation process. Organizations cannot rely on one measure. Rather, ethics must be built into the complex web of its daily operations—it must be part of the system. If it is incorporated into just one area, it risks being overridden and overlooked by pressures of other procedures. A climate of ethics allows employees to do their jobs in a way that most benefits the business. A climate of ethics has a clearly planned reward system—where the right behaviors are being rewarded.

Hackett commented on the wider significance of company actions. "Our efforts to earn our shareholders' trust extend beyond our employees. The Anadarko board of directors' audit committee is charged with understanding, and more importantly, approving of the company's reserve base and reporting system in the same way they are required by regulation to understand and approve the financial reporting," he said, adding: "Our audit committee chair is a petroleum engineer by trade and an industry advocate for better understanding of reserves estimation—his expertise has proven invaluable to our process."

It stands out that Anadarko's attention to its reserve estimation process is not only internally beneficial, it also speaks to the larger environment where other companies have similar internal and external reporting challenges. Anadarko's system also advances toward the higher goal of transparency by satisfying customers, employees, community members, shareholders, and other stakeholders. Trust and investor confidence are key. "Reserve determination is an inexact science, as we don't know with certainty what a field will produce until we actually produce it," Hackett stated. "To instill confidence amongst our investors in our estimation process, we must apply science within a framework of ethical forward thinking."

Hackett also commented on the options open to the industry and what, in his opinion (and in the opinion of their investors) is the best approach. "Some in our industry believe the reserve estimation process should be outsourced for objectivity and validity," he observed. "Nothing could be further from the right approach. While we welcome an outsider looking over our shoulder, there is no substitute for internal competence and integrity. Our investors should want the people estimating reserves to be the employees and management who will lose their jobs, and perhaps their freedom, if they are not prudent.

"An outside firm simply loses a client if they mess up," he explained. "Investors should never want to have management blaming outsiders for incorrect financial or asset statements. We want the arrows pointed directly at those charged with the fiduciary duty of running their enterprises in a responsible manner. That is the management team of those enterprises."

Like other companies in our study, Anadarko realizes that the stakes are higher if the onus is on its own people and organization, yet it embraces the challenge and retains control of the estimation process while welcoming onlookers. Keeping reserve estimation an internal task means risking more in terms of reputation should something go wrong, yet Anadarko is confident in their employees and confers upon them this all-important task.

The Umbrella of the Right Corporate Culture

Reserves accounting is one example of one challenge in one industry. "For us in the oil and gas business, it's a continuously evolving challenge filled with debate, which I believe makes for a better process and stronger industry," Hackett pointed out. "Every business can easily identify their challenges and discuss for hours what they are doing to meet shareholder expectations. Ethics must be part of that discussion. It should be the first sentence of that discussion."

Hackett underlines the importance of a culture that allows ethics to flourish. "The science, technology, business strategy, and delivery are all integral parts to being productive, but they must come together under the umbrella of the right corporate culture," he noted. "This umbrella will help employees make good decisions. Letting your employees do what they know is the right thing to do sounds simpler than it is. But it is the key to creating successful companies where people want to work, and all stakeholders can get excited about the benefits of that business to our larger society."

Like other CEOs concerned about building a climate of ethics, Hackett addressed not only internal issues but also issues facing the wider industry. Ultimately, attention to ethics means better business and benefits to the wider society.

A Primary Responsibility to Society to Do Our Job Well

Rex W. Tillerson, Chairman and CEO of ExxonMobil Corporation emphasizes how seriously it takes its responsibility to society. The company defines its mission as reaching far beyond the actual process of providing energy, something that is true of other companies in our study.

"As the world's largest private petroleum and petrochemical company, we believe that our primary responsibility to society is to do our job well," said Tillerson. "We know that we cannot be all things to all people. Many other organizations—cultural, economic, and political—affect society in ways that are far more consequential than ours. Nevertheless, we recognize that by playing a role in providing high quality energy commodities for a growing world economy, we are helping improve living conditions for millions of people throughout the world."

ExxonMobil's flexibility of mindset is remarkable. It first sees its ethical role as reaching beyond its product, and second, in its ability to say humbly, "we cannot be all things to all people" while broadening its role from providing energy to improving living conditions for millions worldwide.

Tillerson, like other community-minded CEOs in our study, discussed his company's approach. "We also recognize the public's interest in the many ways that we affect the communities and societies where we have operations," he said. "In managing the Corporation's global operations, we work to ensure that our operations are safe, reliable, and environmentally responsible. Our Operations Integrity Management System provides a consistent and disciplined framework to identify, understand, and control risks across our diverse operations worldwide.

"ExxonMobil has shown that we can produce energy and chemical products while protecting the safety and health of people and safeguarding the environment," he explained. "Our goal is no injuries, illnesses, or operational incidents—ultimately fostering a work environment where nobody gets hurt."

Thus, a climate of ethics incorporates a climate of safety into ethical responsibility. It is important to note that ExxonMobil's definition of their role in society is not static. It does not limit the company to merely providing energy. Rather, Tillerson's comment about "improving living conditions" underlines a continuing challenge beyond the company's role as an energy provider.

"ExxonMobil is taking a number of significant actions, as we have for many years, to improve our efficiency and reduce the environmental impact of our operations and in customer use of our products," Tillerson continued. "Improvements are driven by our Global

Energy Management System to help identify and implement energy saving steps at ExxonMobil facilities. A key energy-saving practice is our growing use of cogeneration, the simultaneous production of steam and electricity using clean-burning natural gas. Cogeneration is nearly twice as efficient as traditional methods of producing steam and power separately."

ExxonMobil supplements its internal environmental research and development through cooperative efforts with universities and research centers, as well as through partnerships with other corporations. The emphasis is on learning more about the potential risks of climate change and developing better ways to meet the world's future energy needs. "A notable example," Tillerson said, "is our $100 million investment in Stanford University's Global Climate and Energy Project, a 10-year, $225 million research program aimed at addressing future energy requirements with approaches that can lead to lower greenhouse-gas emissions.

"Our company has a long tradition of helping develop prosperous and stable communities in areas where we operate," Tillerson notes. "The ExxonMobil Foundation is the primary philanthropic arm of the Corporation. The Corporation and its affiliates engage in a broad range of activities focusing on communities where the company has significant operations." In 2005, Tillerson said, company affiliates and the ExxonMobil Foundation combined to provide more than $100 million in charitable contributions and community development investments. More than a third of the total was dedicated to education.

ExxonMobil formulated a far-reaching interpretation of ethics and its ethical responsibilities. It not only pays attention to how it operates its day to day business, it is also concerned with helping society. It gives back in different ways, especially in community development and education. By making donations to university research centers, ExxonMobil tries to anticipate the world's future energy needs, help cure disease and improve community life and education. It is clear how strongly the company identifies its business with a much larger purpose.

"The continuing health crises in developing countries is another challenge where ExxonMobil investments are helping address critical needs, particularly in Africa," Tillerson said. "As a significant and growing investor in sub-Saharan Africa, we have witnessed first hand the impact of malaria on our workforce, their families, and the communities where we operate. At least 300 million people worldwide are afflicted by acute symptoms of the disease. One million people die of malaria every year and about 90 percent of those deaths occur in the sub-Saharan region.

"That is why ExxonMobil has invested more than $11.5 million in grants for malaria prevention, treatment, and research since 2000," he noted. "We believe that improving health in Africa is good for the African economy, good for the African people, and good for companies such as ours that do business in the region and have a long-term commitment to Africa's future."

Tillerson underlined the timelessness of ethics: "The ethical values we inherited from previous generations have lost none of their meaning or importance in today's global economy," he affirmed. "Ethical conduct in business or any other endeavor is vital to the preservation of our free society. Through a steadfast reliance on the values, policies, and practices that have produced favorable results for more than a century, ExxonMobil remains committed to ethical conduct and corporate citizenship."

Tillerson's comments exemplify a key finding from our study: the timeless and enduring nature of ethical values, in this case set in a wider context. He recognizes that ethical values are timeless, and his company's initiatives recognize this timelessness. The contexts and ways in which the values are applied may change, but the core meaning behind them lives on. More importantly, the ethical practices and approaches of yesterday are applicable even in situations that may present themselves differently today. Tillerson's comments show us that not only is ExxonMobil's ethical stance internally focused on aligning employee behavior (as discussed in the previous chapter), but that it is also focused on doing greater good for communities and giving attention to health-related issues.

By setting these examples for employees and organizations involved with its philanthropic donations, ExxonMobil is also shaping the ethical views of others—and their concepts of individual and ethical responsibility. ExxonMobil's commitment to ethical conduct and corporate citizenship is evidenced by how it personally defines its scope of responsibility as an organization. It goes far beyond mechanical code-based compliance by proactively shaping the relationship of business ethics and society.

Often ethical challenges are embedded in the environment and have broader implications for the organization and for wider society. The companies highlighted in this chapter show us how ethically alert organizations use business challenges particular to their industry to be ethically proactive. This leads to benefits for the company as well as the community at large.

Organizations with high ethical awareness see their own ethical contributions as something more than affecting their business; they see them as a contribution to the wider community. Similarly, as will be seen in the next chapter, ethical CEOs look to the wider society when sharing their perspectives on cultivating ethics. They consider the role of ethics education and the business community in spreading a culture of ethics.

Chapter 6

Addressing Future Generations

LEADERS CONCERNED ABOUT ethics must turn their attention to future generations of business professionals. Corporate ethics are a reflection on the business community and the role of business in society. Ethical leaders talk about governance, regulation, and the reputation of the industry. In reaching audiences inside and outside the firm, CEOs discuss their challenges to ensure that ethical energy is transferred to those who will carry organizations, institutions, and communities into the future. CEOs must attend to the need to address ethics in the educational arena and ensure that it evolves and continues.

Trust as the Great Intangible Necessary for True, Long-Term Success

Edward B. Rust Jr.,[1] Chairman and CEO of State Farm, pays special attention to tomorrow's businesspeople. He takes a comprehensive

---

[1]The material we received from Mr. Rust for this chapter is based on a speech he gave to the AACSB—Association to Advance Collegiate Schools of Business-International in April 2005.

view of what it means to uphold ethics in society. It requires that educators and leaders work together. Although major symbolic structures have recently endured ethical compromises and tarnished images, it is our responsibility—and that of future leaders and current students—to continue to build a society of trust and honesty.

Rust first looks at the impact of scandals and ways to restore confidence and trust. His comments highlight the need for leaders to play an exemplary role in demonstrating ethical behavior and calling attention to ethics. He envisions the positive outcome of business leaders and educators joining forces.

"The world economic system is built on a cornerstone of trust," said Rust. "Recent years' string of ethical failures in business has weakened this cornerstone and subsequently jeopardized our economic future. Meanwhile, the very institutions people turn to for reassurance and to shore up their moral values have also been tarnished. Our governments, colleges and universities, even some of our religious institutions, have been plagued with scandals."

These failures have shaken public confidence, Rust believes. "There's a sense that our nation's values and ethical behavior are on the decline and that our trust in one another is weakening," he observed. "All of this comes at a time when the public also feels less secure physically and economically. The real threat of terrorism has imbedded itself in everyone's lives. Pension benefits are at risk, the future of Social Security is uncertain, medical care and energy costs continue to rise."

The mistrust that has woven its way throughout society, in Rust's view, doesn't have to continue. "Educators have a chance to change the behaviors that erode our ethical and moral standards," he noted. "In partnership with business leaders, they have an opportunity to restore and rebuild the trust that is so important to our way of life."

This opportunity begins anew each fall when colleges and universities open their doors to an incoming freshman class. As Rust explained: "When they arrive on campus, these students' moral compasses may be oriented, but they're not set. Higher education can impact their values and behavior in powerful and lasting ways."

Rust quoted a 2005 op-ed piece in the *New York Times* by Yale University professor Robert Shiller: "Education molds not just individuals but also common assumptions and conventional wisdom. And when it comes to the business world, our universities—and especially their graduate business schools—are powerful shapers of the culture."

The culture to which Shiller refers dominates formal rules and policies and dictates choices students make. "Because so many college graduates with non-business degrees find careers in business," Rust said, "it's imperative that all schools, not just business schools, emphasize integrity and assume more responsibility for shaping a culture of solid and unbendable ethics and moral values."

Rust thinks that an ethics curriculum should be embedded in all coursework and not isolated to a specific class. "Ethical issues won't come at these students isolated from a set of circumstances," he said. "There are no clear signs posted along life's highways that warn of an approaching ethical dilemma or moral choice."

It is of primary importance, according to Rust, for education to illuminate "the reality that in business there is tremendous pressure exerted by boards, stockholders, owners and employees for companies to grow and be profitable." In this constant quest for profits, he said, "people lose sight of the fact that business moves in cycles.

Instead of breaking rules to eliminate them, we need to remind ourselves that cycles are a fact of life, and that no matter how dire circumstances may seem, we have to maintain standards and trust. Society's trust in our economic system, and the resulting long-term shareholder value, can't lose out to the lust for short-term paper profits."

Rust turns to messages that put ethical choices at risk. "Business leaders routinely urge their teams to do 'whatever it takes' to meet their goals and 'hit their numbers.' Even when strong ethics are present at the highest levels of leadership, this message can get distorted as it cascades down through an organization," he observed. "There is a real danger that this message will be interpreted literally as an order without conditions and limitations, as a license to push the boundaries of internal guidelines and the law and, if necessary, to quietly cross those boundaries." It's all too easy for people to modify and rationalize their behavior when under pressure and faced with difficult circumstances. This is especially the case, said Rust, "when there's honor in being branded as someone willing to do 'whatever it takes' to get the job done."

Rust focuses on another reality in today's business environment. "Ethics are harder to ensure in a world where companies have ballooned in size and have crossed political and cultural boundaries," he commented. Establishing and maintaining accountability is much more of a challenge, in his view, because of the size, power, and influence of corporations and their leaders.

Rust considered the role of educators in contributing to a culture of ethics in the business world, saying, "In addition to helping students understand and appreciate these realities, educators can reinforce some basic premises that will help them form their own solid cornerstone of integrity." He addresses students and future leaders about what, in his view, can be taught:

- **You control your environment:** When you enter the job market, it's your responsibility to take some measure of a prospective employer's sense of ethics, and learn how that business responds when there's a breach. Do the values of the company align with your personal values? If not, are you willing to compromise those values to work there?
- **Actions have consequences:** Bad behavior will put you, your family, your fellow employees, company shareholders, and even your community at risk. Once you've crossed the line of moral and ethical behavior, it's hard to make a U-turn.
- **Actions speak louder than words:** People watch which activity is rewarded and which behavior is recognized. Leaders who say one thing but do another send a loud and conflicting message. Building and reinforcing a culture that rejects unethical behavior and consistently rewards people for doing the right thing is critical to the survival of individual businesses and our society. As a future business leader, you're responsible for fostering and developing a culture where asking difficult questions is not only permissible, but encouraged.
- **Take time to reflect:** Business leaders must dedicate time [to remove themselves] from the day-to-day, hour by hour operations [so they can] reflect on the big picture. It gives them time to think, and ultimately understand, the realities of their own world.

- **Seek counsel:** It's very helpful to have someone who can serve as a sounding board on moral issues. If you're hesitant or embarrassed to describe a situation to someone else, then you may already have your answer. The more success you attain and the higher you rise within an organization, the more likely the people around you will try to protect you from unpleasant issues. This isolation will limit your views, insights, and perspective.

  Many of the people who have been ensnared in the public spotlight of questionable ethics were at the top of their fields. They lost sight of the fact that their personal actions and their decisions were being judged on Main Street as well as Wall Street. Either they chose to ignore the ethical storms brewing on the horizon or they surrounded themselves with people whose forecasts were unrealistic and overly optimistic.

- **Real life is full of real lessons:** The most effective lessons won't be learned discussing theories and hypotheses. There are all too many real-life examples readily available for teaching purposes. Employers put a high value on graduates who are able to apply critical thinking skills. There's no better way to build these skills than through regular classroom discussion of actual ethical dilemmas and transgressions.

- **There are lessons in both success and failure:** Educators and business leaders are quick to applaud and eager to call attention to successful graduates and colleagues. It delivers a valuable lesson when we spotlight the success of those who made the right choices and then were rewarded for them. There are also lessons to be learned in talking about those who made the wrong choices. We need to seriously discuss and dissect their real-life stories and analyze the decisions they made. Some of them might be willing to share their experiences and life-learnings. Powerful is the lesson taught at the hands of someone who's experienced the pain and embarrassment of an ethical lapse firsthand. In balance, we should call attention to those people who recognized unethical and illegal behaviors and instead of turning their heads, raised their hands and spoke up.

These classroom exercises force students to confront the issues and realize what can happen when they cross the line. During these discussions, students should consider whether there are exceptions to blanket decisions, and whether the ethics line is bright and unbending. Students—with the help of their teachers—should analyze the "gray areas" of ethics, a topic that allows plenty of room for debate and discussion.

- **The Golden Rule:** Some suggest the religious pluralism and cultural divisiveness so present in today's society makes teaching basic values in our classrooms difficult, if not impossible. We need to overcome this and acknowledge that the Golden Rule—"do unto others as you would have them do unto you"—is a moral precept found in virtually every religion. It is a solid benchmark for ethical values.

- **Short-term pain for long-term gain:** An important fact that today's students and tomorrow's business leaders must know (but one that's difficult to appreciate) is that even though following the rules will serve you well in the long term, it sometimes puts you at a short-term disadvantage. Choosing to do the right thing does not always lead to immediate and recognizable success. Albert Einstein said, "Not everything that counts can be counted." Applied to business, the lesson in his words is that even though it's easier to measure assets, liabilities, and quarterly performance than it is to quantify honesty and trustworthiness, the economic prosperity we enjoy requires trust.

- **Give back to the community:** Finally, students should be encouraged to become involved in public service as volunteers and interns. This valuable work helps students gain perspective and it will instill in them strong values and ethics. It will place them in situations where they can explore commitments that go beyond themselves.

  Rust calls for everyone to contribute. "The path that leads to strong ethics is lined with good values and proper behavior. Everyone has a responsibility to help the leaders of tomorrow develop the moral muscle that will keep them on this path, even when they're pushed against its boundaries," he stressed. "Tomorrow's business people must know that it's possible to succeed and maintain their moral values. They must understand that ethics and integrity are not just concepts, but are the very real foundation for our own economic and social survival."

Leaving a Legacy and Looking to the Future

Richard L. Keyser, Chairman and CEO of W.W. Grainger, Inc., chooses to address future leaders when asked about his perspectives on ethics in business. "I was a member of the Naval Academy Class of 1964," he said. "Upon graduation, rather than give a typical class gift, like a park bench, we wanted our legacy to have a more practical application. So we created a fund to support the writing of a book, *Ethics for the Junior Officer*, which deals with situations young officers might encounter. We also established an endowment to fund updates to the book. Every year, representatives from our class return to the Academy and speak to the graduating midshipmen, each of whom receives a copy."

In talking about the past, Keyser gave an example of forward-looking behavior: his class passed on a legacy to future classes at the Naval Academy. Its vintage signifies the importance of ethics over time, with the charge carried on for each graduate. "It's a terrific program, and I understand the book is viewed as a rich resource for self-study, analysis, and reflection," he continued. "I'm pleased that the Academy recognizes its merits and that today, some 40 years later, the school now operates a Center for the Study of Professional Military Ethics."

The Center is not alone. "These days, the topic of ethics is being addressed in the classroom more and more, but can ethics really be taught? I'm not sure," he says. "We can certainly cite examples of good and bad behavior. We can coach people in how to reason through a dilemma. But ultimately, it comes down to the individual's sense of right and wrong. Therefore, I think the best thing that families and schools and even companies can do is instill a sense of pride in doing the right thing, regardless of the circumstances. We need to give young people—all people, actually—the courage to make the tough choices when the decisions aren't easy."

Keyser underlined the importance of a context that nurtures ethical awareness. The individual is at the center and placed in a context—whether it is family, school, or company—where mentors help develop individuals' sense of right and wrong and energize them to *want* to do what is right. In the end it is the individual who makes the final choice.

"There are a lot of reasons to behave ethically in business, but most boil down to the fact that doing what's right is just good business," said Keyser. "You could call it an enlightened self-interest. My company, Grainger, supplies businesses and institutions with the products they need to keep their facilities running. Our operating philosophy is built around service. It always has been. We stand behind our promises."

Keyser gives examples illustrating trust and loyalty. "For example, we are careful about paying our bills on time, a trait that makes our suppliers respect us. Our customers are loyal because we treat them fairly. A deal's a deal, even if it's painful in the short term."

He describes an example: "A few years ago, we had a bid on a large contract and the employee drawing up the bid priced the products way too low. So of course we got the contract. I'll admit it: that hurt. But we held up our end of the bargain, even though the mistake made it difficult for us to make any money on that contract. It was the right thing to do." The company stood by this bid and it also stood by the employee, who is still with the company.

Keyser's broad definition of "doing the right thing" is clear, as it is with other companies in our study. As he stated himself, "we also go the extra mile to treat our employees fairly and with dignity. It doesn't cost that much more, and the goodwill it breeds can yield big dividends. On average, people will change jobs seven to 10 times during their careers, and—who knows?—many of our employees could become customers some day."

Keyser posed a question to students and future leaders: "Chances are good that in the coming years, you'll find yourself in a leadership position. How will you ensure that the organizations you join will continue to operate ethically?"

His response was: "I believe that it comes from individual action. It's difficult for companies, who hire from society at large, to instill a strong ethical norm throughout the organization, but my sense is that most people want to work in that kind of an environment, and that given the opportunity most will look for ways to encourage it." Recognizing the challenge of instilling a climate of ethics, Keyser once again emphasized the importance of an environment that encourages individuals to act ethically.

"At Grainger, we articulate proper behavior in training programs and in our Business Conduct Guidelines, which employees must sign every year," he explains. Those guidelines provide the parameters, he said, "but rules mean little unless they're supported by values. Tough as it may be, our leadership has to demonstrate that we will take action, without exception, for a breach of conduct. Even our best sales rep would be fired if he or she were caught cheating on expense reports. Stealing a little is no better and no worse than stealing a lot.

"Equally important, we try very hard to encourage and recognize employees who do the right thing," he continued, "We want everyone to be willing to step up to the plate and admit to their bosses, as our employee did, that he'd made a mistake on his bid and consequently would miss his budget; and that even though it might mean losing his job, he thought the company should stand behind the bid. We did, and we stood by him as well. He's still with Grainger.

"I'm not saying that these are easy actions to take, but if you don't, who will?" he asked. "Ethics are about individuals and the choices each of us make, so as you head back to your projects or your day-to-day activities, consider this: Did you ever borrow a particularly choice phrase to use in a report? Take credit for an idea that wasn't wholly your own? Embellish your résumé? Being ethical in your work starts now, before you join—or rejoin—the ranks of corporate America."

Keyser's comments underline "being ethical" as the sum of individuals' ethical actions. It doesn't just happen on its own: It must be a personal contribution from everyone, in business and in society— rooted in nurturing one's sense of right and wrong.

That "Somebody Is Us"

Henry L. Meyer, CEO of KeyCorp, addressed an audience about business ethics and reform:[2] "People, not companies, make decisions. People, not governments, make decisions. People, not computers, make decisions. Ethics is about the everyday decisions and actions of people just like you and me."

---

[2]Speech text delivered by Henry L. Meyer III, Chairman and CEO, KeyCorp (2004). This section draws on parts of the speech.

While recognizing there is a long way to go in instilling ethics throughout business and society, Meyer chose to take a positive approach, saying, "Fortunately, there's a lot we can do to help." He shared what he calls "just two of many steps forward that we can take to reform business further.

"First, let's expand business ethics education. As I've stated before, I believe that people are born with a moral compass, but that compass needs ongoing calibration, because new and unfamiliar situations arise all the time," he noted. "One hundred years ago, for instance, businesses didn't have to wrestle with the implications of nuclear power, the Internet, or human cloning. Today, many do. Properly tuned, a moral compass helps people do the right thing in any difficult situation, business related or otherwise."

Meyer's comments underline a key theme: ethical development is ongoing and relies greatly on keeping a moral compass "properly tuned." People need tools when challenged by an unusual circumstance or a new perplexity in business. The moral compass evolves with the individual thanks to ethical initiatives, whether within a company or in education.

With this example we can picture the energy around ethics as an actively developing asset, necessary on an individual as well as collective level. However, being ethical—providing foundations—is a responsibility that goes beyond the individual manager or company. Educators are also involved. Actions must be viewed as contributing to a greater environmental or social cause.

"Business ethics training can help by having people examine situations from multiple perspectives. This includes helping students to envision consequences—both good and bad," said Meyer. "It exposes them, through discussions with others, to a variety of humane responses to tough issues. Finally, business ethics training can help by creating positive peer pressure. We should never assume that a person, by virtue of age or experience, cannot be influenced to be better."

Meyer noted the advantages of ethics training in a collective atmosphere, and points out that the first course in business ethics was offered by the Harvard Business School in 1915. "But," he added, "the topic didn't become a mainstream offering in business schools until the mid-1980s, when a string of corporate scandals highlighted the need. Perhaps you remember Ivan Boesky and Michael Milken."

Unfortunately, many people still question the benefits of ethics education, Meyer said. He referred to a 2002 survey of top corporate ethics officers conducted by the business research organization the Conference Board,[3] which indicated that a majority of respondents thought that, even if Enron's senior management had received extensive ethics training, it would have made little or no difference in preventing what happened.

"Why do they feel that way?" asked Meyer. His answer: "Part of it lies in the way business schools have traditionally tackled ethics education. Most hired ethics instructors trained in the fields of philosophy and religion. These people were passionate and well-meaning, but they tended to be theoretical, asking, for instance: Is capitalism ethically justifiable? They tended to use language alien to

---

[3]The Conference Board is an organization supported by corporate contributions that offers a variety of services, including research. It calculates the Leading Index for the United States and has a vast array of information on ethics.

business students, and to us, for that matter. Just how are we to discuss 'deontology' or 'utilitarianism' at tomorrow's staff meeting?

"Finally, the ethics instructors tended to stress moral absolutes," Meyer said. "For instance: If ethical behavior leads to a company's demise, oh well. In other words, their instruction wasn't terribly practical."

Meyer's comments underline the need for ethics to be taught using common language and a practical approach.

Meyer identified another problem: "Companies have typically sought business graduates who have mastered 'harder' skills such as finance, market research, and operations management. 'Softer' skills, such as moral reasoning, have been deemed less useful. They are not. Soft skills are what CEOs and other leaders are really all about. I assure you: Ethical leaders are as tough as nails.

"Our first task, then, is to get practical about business ethics education," Meyer continued. He presented "four simple ways we can do so":

First, we can become students ourselves by reading up on ethics. There are many fine books available to help you expand your understanding.

Second, we can develop our ethics muscle by talking with people about what we've read. You'd be amazed to hear the varied and constructive ideas they have—ideas that can inform and improve any business decision we make.

Third, we can teach others the practical skills we master. For instance, we can volunteer to speak at our local high school, college, or university. We can offer to help shape the curricula of professional or trade associations to which we belong. We can serve as a mentor to young people who are just starting their careers. It will be time well spent.

Finally, we can probe harder when establishing new relationships, especially when hiring or selecting people. Let's make sure that candidates possess more than just the technical skills needed to fulfill a role. Let's interview for character.

The responsibility of leaders to play an ethical role in society comes through in many of the points made by Meyer as he addresses students, business leaders, and educators. For Meyer, ethics involves personal decisions. Individuals all contribute to an ethical environment. The moral compass needs ongoing calibration to deal with new situations. One's sense of right and wrong must evolve, and to evolve there must be a continuous dialogue, enriched by a variety of viewpoints to trigger one's own development. Meyer turns to the second step for reforming business further. It is to expect more from all the participants in our economic system, which will be detailed in our concluding chapter.

Recognizing and Rewarding Ethical Behavior

Curt S. Culver, CEO of MGIC Investment Corp., shares the importance of upbringing and applying simple rules to business life. Laws are not the solution to solving ethical quagmires: He prefers to set the example and tone at the top. He delivered a speech about the Better Business Bureau's Torch Awards in 2004 to an audience that included finalists and employees. He first congratulated the 10 finalists for being recognized "for outstanding business ethics and integrity" and continued by discussing ethics.

Culver, like many other CEOs intent on encouraging a culture of ethics, draws on his family background. "Craig[4] and I were fortunate to have been raised in a family business where honesty, integrity, and quality were ingrained in everything we did," he said. "And I'm proud to say that Craig has carried on that tradition with Culver's. Our parents, by example, taught us that principles are as important to people as roots are to trees. Without them, you can't survive. Honesty, integrity, respect, [and] fairness all matter and make a difference in how you run your business and most importantly, how you live your life." Culver stressed the importance of building strong foundations and then supporting them.

Culver, however, feels that "somehow, particularly in the public company arena, we seem to have gotten away from these principles and, as a result, the integrity of corporate America is being questioned today as it had not been since the Great Depression.

"The sorry state of affairs that prevailed at Enron, Tyco, World-Com, HealthSouth, and a host of other companies that costs investors trillions of dollars," he said, "was an embarrassment to all publicly traded companies. And even more galling to me was the fact that in most of these instances the CEOs and other members of

---

[4]Mr. Culver's older brother was present at the event. The Torch Awards, Better Business Bureau, were held on October 13, 2004.

management walked away with hundreds of millions of dollars from stock sales, as their employees lost their jobs and their life savings.

"So, the question is: what do we do about these scandals to prevent them in the future?" he asked. "Frequently, the reaction to a problem is 'we need new laws, we need new codes of conduct.' And laws have certainly been passed, as evidenced by the Sarbanes-Oxley Act two years ago, the most sweeping corporate reform legislation in 60 years that all but three members of Congress voted for—that's a problem, as is the fact that it took only 10 days to pass. Bipartisan."

Culver continued: "But to me, the key safeguard is not laws, but rather it is the integrity of management. *You cannot legislate integrity.* When you try to implement new laws or rules, you end up legislating additional costs and providing great work for lawyers."

Culver provided an example: "For instance, when all is said and done, Sarbanes-Oxley implementation will probably cost our company $2.6 million. And I say probably, because it could be more—and we are a simple company. In addition, it has clearly been a distraction to our coworkers. It has significantly raised our directors' fees, our D&O insurance, our outside audit fees, and it will probably limit the pool of director availability. It clearly is swatting a fly with a sledge hammer. And for what?"

Culver stressed that the behavior of individuals is key. Such behavior must be taken into account in initiatives and measures that on their own might not contribute to ethical behavior. "The bad actors at Enron, Tyco, WorldCom and others are all being prosecuted under laws that have long existed," he explained. "Each of these companies had wonderfully written audit committee charters, and they also had great sets of corporate governance principles. So it's not what is on the piece of paper that's important, but rather, it's how people act on a day-to-day basis. That's why succession planning for the CEO is one of the most important duties of the Board. It is the CEO who sets the tone. He or she is the key to emphasizing integrity and doing what's right."

Culver specified that his words do not dismiss recent legislation. "But don't get me totally wrong. Sarbanes-Oxley has made some positive changes. For instance, the new Public Company Accounting Oversight Board should stiffen the resolve of auditors to resist management pressure for reporting that is too aggressive.

"I am also not concerned about the CEO certifications," he added. "At MGIC, we have also taken our disclosure obligations very seriously. Also, I think the prohibition on personal loans was necessary. There's no reason for any company to lend the CEO millions of dollars to buy stock. And the faster reporting of Director and Officer stock transactions is also a positive. But again I come back to: *at what cost?*"

Culver's comments show that he attributes great importance to the integrity of the management team in conjunction with strong Board of Director practices that provide integrity to the process and protection for shareholders. Culver summarized his view of what's important for excellent corporate governance:

1. Good people running the company. (Remember, you can't legislate integrity.)

2. Boards that have good processes to oversee those people.

3. And finally, an area that I haven't talked about, but which is the ultimate safeguard: an enforcement agency (i.e., the SEC) that has the resources to regulate financial filings in a timely manner.

"If these three principles of governance are followed, SOX will become an exercise rather than a necessity," said Culver, using an abbreviation for Sarbanes-Oxley. "It's just sad that the financial abuses of a few imposed such a cost on us all. Just as importantly, it cast my profession in a very bad light, which is not the case at all. At the vast majority of companies in America, I guarantee the CEO cares more about the people that work for them than he does about his or her own livelihood. Trust me, you feel a tremendous obligation to your coworkers.

"You will also see, as evidenced by our community, that no one cares more about their community than CEOs," he continues. "I see this day in and day out, where people give of their time and financial resources to make this a better community. And none of them asks for anything in return other than the satisfaction that they know they did the right thing. We are fortunate to have so many who care so much for this community."

This example underlines that more than laws or a new codes of ethics are needed. It is the CEO and people at all levels of the organization who must focus on integrity and set an example in doing what is right.

Setting High Ethical Standards

Alan B. Miller, Chairman, CEO, and President of Universal Health Services (UHS), underlines the role of leaders in setting ethical standards. "Over the past several years, business ethics has become a hot topic, mostly because there have been some high profile corporate implosions, indictments, and convictions," he said. "Sometimes it takes these types of incidents to initiate meaningful change. To its credit, Congress has responded to all of this by toughening the disclosure and financial reporting standards for public companies, and using their bully pulpit to publicly embarrass and chastise unethical business leaders. And my guess is that government may get more involved in the coming years, which shouldn't be viewed as a bad thing for corporate America.

"But while Congress, the SEC, and other governmental bodies undoubtedly play an important role in legislating corporate governance standards and ethical behavior," he continued, "I firmly believe that corporate leaders have a duty to set the highest ethical standards for their companies. Employees take their cues from their corporate leaders. If they see managers cutting corners, operating in 'gray areas,' or otherwise acting inappropriately, it leaves the impression that this type of behavior is permissible. And eventually this type of behavior pervades the company. In that sense, actions speak much louder than words."

In Miller's words, we can see the vital role that leaders play as ethical exemplars. Leading by example and mentoring places a greater responsibility on leaders in the business world—not only in leading their corporations, but also in embracing their exemplary role. It is the social responsibility of the leader on a personal level.

"It's also important to keep in mind that just because something is legal doesn't mean it's ethical," Miller pointed out. "Legal standards are derived from the law. Ethical standards are derived from a higher morality and character. If your business practices or ethics simply mirror the bare minimum legal requirements and mandates, invariably there will be 'gray-area situations' where that line gets crossed occasionally, whether intentional or unintentional.

"There's less chance of this happening when business practices are grounded in something other than legal requirements, such as a sense of right and wrong," he continued. "It's not just enough to ask if a certain behavior is legal. The real questions are: Is this right or is this wrong? Does this behavior exhibit the values we strive to embody? Does it reflect our character? Is it consistent with our corporate culture? The answers to these questions should reflect a higher ethical standard than the simple legal requirements."

We can see a key message here. Set the standards very high. Go to the maximum so that the minimum cannot be so bare. In essence, corporations should aim to be proactive and exemplary on the ethics front—it is not enough to just be ethical this year or this quarter. It should be ongoing and evolving to meet new challenges.

"I'm not sure if ethics and strong character is a learned behavior or an innate instinct. That's probably for someone else to determine," said Miller. "I was fortunate to have my father as my role model. He was the most honest person I've ever known. There was never any gray area with him—things were either right or wrong, plain and simple. For aspiring business leaders, the most important advice I can give is to find a strong role model—someone who reflects the values and character you admire—and learn from them. And surround yourself with like-minded individuals. In the long run, it will benefit yourself and your company."

Many of the CEOs whose thoughts appear in these chapters have underlined the role of the leader in exemplifying ethical behavior, with ethics reinforced via schools and the wider society. Moreover, ethics must be a part of the individual. The charge rests with the individual facing a situation and making the right and moral choice. Ethical decisions need to be made in situations that may present themselves differently than they appear in codes of conduct, rules, or law. Our personal moral compass is always evolving and being more finely tuned. The concluding chapter moves toward the societal dimension and the energetic charge towards ethics.

Chapter 7

Making Ethics Contagious

BY RELENTLESSLY COMMUNICATING about ethics and taking a range of initiatives, ethical CEOs and their companies are actually helping to make ethics contagious. They do this when they build an ethical climate in their organizations. They do this when they take a "big picture" view of ethics in business. By their actions and their words, these CEOs underscore the need for ethical behavior to be widespread, beyond the single company and throughout society and the industry.

A climate of ethics must pervade the organization and be part of its culture. While core values remain a solid foundation, ethical initiatives evolve to meet changing contexts. Ethical energy has life of its own. It is not something that comes into being at a fixed point in time. Ethical CEOs use multiple methods to keep enthusiasm about ethics high. They recognize that formal codes, however important they are, cannot on their own create an honest organization. Leaders need to exemplify ethical behavior, but at the same time ethics is not "owned" by one level of the organization. Individuals need to feel they are charged with the responsibility. Honest organizations aim to go beyond compliance. They define "doing the right thing" in very broad terms to raise expectations.

Building a culture of ethics also means focusing attention on learning, both within the organization and across wider society. The challenge of ethics education is to make people—who have not yet experienced real-life dilemmas—aware of what underlies ethical decision-making. Difficult cases can be studied and can become a springboard to help strengthen the ethical base of a company. With the ethics of the business world at issue, corporations, associations, and educational institutions need to work together to encourage a widespread culture of ethics.

Ethical CEOs help develop the ethical character of the organization. But the ethical vision must encompass a responsibility to overall society, not just a customer or a supervisor or a company. Actions must be viewed as contributing to a greater environmental or social cause.

Several key themes have emerged from our study. CEOs entrusted with building honest organizations own the challenge of coordinating a vast variety of efforts. They must energize their individual human resources toward the greater goal of accomplishing business ethically.

Chapter by chapter, we have reported on our analysis and laid out the key approaches that CEOs use to build ethics in their organizations. The emerging theme at the core of all these approaches rests upon bringing ethics to the individual. This requires a crisp and clear understanding of ethics—a common interpretation among employees that is applicable to a variety of contexts. CEOs are faced with the arduous task of ensuring that all actions toward ethical goals converge at a common understanding of what it means to be ethical.

CEOs have a repertoire of practices to ensure this common understanding, from telling stories to using challenges to galvanize employees and build unity. CEOs use tangible artifacts such as written codes, but they also rely on such intangibles as culture, history, and traditions. CEOs ensure their messages endure by using multiple channels to spread their word—channels that retain messages and create ethical archives.

CEOs create ethical energy, which needs to flow outside of the boundaries of their organizations. CEOs make their visions of ethics, their practices, and their efforts far-reaching. They are alert to the impressions that their actions will leave on their peers, as well as on individuals rising to positions of power or newcomers just entering the professional world. In this regard, CEOs strive to inspire not only those they work with, but also students, businesses, peers, regulators, researchers, the community at large, and those in search of new ethical ideas. CEOs have an unspoken responsibility to expand the ethical horizon and build an ever more solid foundation for others.

In this concluding chapter, we present some final perspectives of CEOs as they reflect on wider issues. We also draw on quotes of CEOs from earlier chapters to review the themes developed throughout the book: excitement and enthusiasm, stories that keep values alive, the importance of reputation, giving to communities, and awareness of the external environment.

Ethical Challenges as Opportunities

Many CEOs in our study reflected on recent scandals but also recognized that attention to ethics is not new to many companies. James T. Hackett, President and CEO of Anadarko Petroleum explained why ethics is good for people and trust essential for business.

"Despite recent years' headlines of misguided corporate decisions, failed companies, and flawed executives, the discussion of ethics in a corporate culture isn't new to this century," he began. "In fact, today's blue chip corporations have learned over decades that through ethical behavior you can produce not only a good product or service, you can also empower employees, create a sense of service to society, and satisfy shareholders who—rightly so—expect you to act with integrity and truthfulness.

"In Wall Street speak, every public company, regardless of its commodity, service, or skill set, exists to provide a competitive and sustainable rate of return to its shareholders, thereby providing a service to society through providing jobs, paying taxes, and satisfying consumer needs," Hackett continued. "For Anadarko Petroleum Corporation, one of the world's largest independent exploration and production companies, our return is based on how well we find and produce oil and natural gas.

"But obviously the relationship between company and shareholder is more complex than just providing value. It's not enough for us, or any corporation, to be merely capable," he explained. "Countless capable companies have fallen not because they couldn't do their job, but because while doing their job, they lost the trust of their shareholders and/or the public. Building and retaining shareholder and public trust, while not as quantitative as cash flow and revenue reports, is just as integral to the company's real and perceived value.

"The difficult task of overseeing corporate behavior falls mostly to the SEC and court system for American companies," said Hackett. "At a minimum, corporations should be in compliance with the law, but how does compliance translate to the daily decisions made by employees? If a corporation's goal is simply to be compliant, it is missing an opportunity to bring itself closer to the ethical expectations of its stakeholders."

Hackett discussed the implication of focusing on compliance only. "Compliance assumes that employees at every level of the corporation will know, understand, and interpret complex laws promulgated domestically and internationally—and stay abreast of changes to same," he explained. "Training classes and employee communications are imperative parts of the equation, but training alone won't make our employees interpreters of the law.

"Integrity, honesty, and ethics cannot be legislated," he emphasized.

A much simpler approach, in his view, is what works: "Hire and retain good people who have the desire to do the right thing and inherently know the right thing to do. Then create a culture that requires, rewards, and models ethical behavior.

"The last of these—demonstrating ethical behavior to employees— is critical. Recent corporate scandals have highlighted the very real need for employees to have a transparent view of their corporation's leaders and their company's decision-making process," he noted. "Management sets the standards that the entire organization will strive to meet. Leaders cannot ignore the fact that employees will follow upper management's lead, not only in business execution, but in ethical behavior as well. We can either see this challenge as problematic or as a tremendous opportunity to lead great organizations."

Hackett underlines the importance of hiring practices and a culture built around ethics, with leaders modeling ethical behavior. Cultures evolve with their organizations and outlast individual employees. Cultures are contagious: a shared culture ensures values, practices, and norms spread to new employees. Newcomers thus become part of the fabric of an organization and they come to share its mindset.

Ethics as Part of a Performance-Driven Culture

Aside from focusing on ethics-related initiatives and his company's foundation, as previously discussed, William (Bill) Nuti, Chairman and CEO of NCR Corporation also takes a broad view in articulating his perspectives. Again, we see how important it is for the CEO to communicate about ethics, values, and integrity. Nuti affirmed that there is "no middle ground" when it comes to ethics, and emphasizes that this position is compatible with a performance-driven culture.

"Working for a company that places such a high priority on doing what's right, even when no one is looking, aligns with my strong belief that when the subject is ethics, there is no middle ground—we must always operate with the highest levels of integrity," said Nuti. "I do believe for a company to be successful, it has to have an externally focused, risk-taking, performance-driven culture. However, having that kind of a culture doesn't mean that you cheat. You always do things the right way."

Success, however, may lead to temptation, he observed: "When things are going well for a company, you have a great deal of momentum and are on a roll. This is often the time when folks are tempted to step over the line."

Nuti's response as a leader was this: "I don't want anyone even *dipping their toe* into the gray area."

Like other CEOs who recognize that leaders may have to overcome hurdles in their quest for an honest organization, Nuti let us in on how he felt personally, in this case regarding troubles that occurred at another company before his appointment there. "While the well-documented problems at Symbol Technologies preceded my arrival as president at that company, I still had to deal with those challenges, and I can tell you personally that it is not a pleasant experience to go through," he recalled. "That's why I see no alternative to adhering to the highest standards of ethics and integrity, both in my personal and professional life. We can't let down our families, employees, shareholders, and other stakeholders who put their trust in our decisions—a responsibility that none of us should ever take lightly."

Nuti highlighted the importance of actions while recognizing that words also contribute to the culture and values of an organization. "Each and every one of us 'sets the tone' for our respective organizations, not only through our words, but mostly through our actions—and inactions," he stated in closing. "Management layers, titles, or geographies do not diminish this simple fact."

Expecting More from Everyone

We understand from the previous chapter that Henry L. Meyer, Chairman and CEO of KeyCorp, considers ethics education a first step towards business reform:[1] "There's a second step forward that we can take to reform business further, and that's to raise the bar by

---

[1]Chapter 6 includes his comments on business education, made in the earlier part of his speech *That 'Somebody' Is Us.* Speech text delivered by Henry L. Meyer III, Chairman and CEO, KeyCorp (2004).

expecting more from all the participants in our economic system."
He continued:

"Imagine a world:

- Where CEOs and other senior executives 'walk the talk'
  when it comes to ethical leadership;
- Where boards and their committees are engaged and
  objective;
- Where analysts evaluate stocks fairly and independently; and
- Where shareholders harbor more reasonable expectations
  about investment returns.

"Imagine a world:

- Where auditing firms view investors as clients;
- Where employees challenge suspect business practices; and
- Where the media showcases positive behaviors—as well as
  continues to expose negative ones."

Meyer turned his attention to new legislation. "I think that many
of the new and proposed legal and regulatory reforms will help. For
instance, I applaud the bans imposed by the Securities and Exchange
Commission and the Sarbanes-Oxley Act," he said. "They prevent
accounting firms from also selling services, such as consulting, to
their clients.

"I also applaud the new listing standards adopted by the
New York Stock Exchange and the Nasdaq. Among other things,
they require firms to get shareholder approval for all stock-option
plans," Meyer continued. "They require firms to have a majority of

independent directors on their boards. And they allow only independent directors on the audit committee and on the committees that select chief executives and determine pay.

"I'm also pleased that The U.S. Sentencing Commission voted unanimously in January of last year to impose stiffer penalties on white-collar criminals;" he said. "In some cases, sentences will double.

"These all are good and appropriate reforms. They're also shareholder-savvy," Meyer explained. "A comprehensive study by GovernanceMetrics International, an independent corporate governance ratings agency, examined the three-year total returns on shares for the period ended March 20, 2003. During that period, the return on the S&P 500 Index overall was a negative 2 percent. The 15 companies with the strongest governance practices averaged a positive 3 percent, with the top 5 companies averaging a positive 23 percent. In contrast, the three-year total return for the 50 companies with the worst governance practices averaged negative 11 percent.

"Yet more reform is needed," said Meyer. "In addition, we need to remember that reforms on paper are meaningless unless they're backed up by thoughtful implementation and vigorous enforcement. Hopefully, people will rise to the occasion.

"Of course, no law or regulation is a substitute for personal commitments by honorable business people to behave ethically," Meyer observed. "Without such commitment, we risk drowning our companies in a sea of rules. And free economies cannot advance if management's discretion becomes too limited or formulaic."

Meyer identifies a vision of an ethical business world where ethics is self-motivated. Ethics dictated by reforms alone are limited. Ethical behavior needs implementation, enforcement, and above all personal commitment.

Future Generations of Leaders

Addressing ethics education, Edward B. Rust Jr.,[2] Chairman and CEO of State Farm, sent a strong message with his closing comments. He makes a call for collective action, creating a sense of shared responsibility toward the future. "Together we must do 'whatever it takes,' without limits and without conditions, to produce a next generation of leaders who understand and believe that trust is the great intangible necessary for true, long-term success," he said. "We need a next generation of leaders prepared to live and lead by example, a next generation dedicated to reinforcing rather than chipping away at the cornerstone of trust that supports our economic system."

A Race without a Finish Line

Winding down her speech at Bentley College Center for Business Ethics,[3] Anne Mulcahy, CEO of Xerox Corporation said, "Social responsibility and business ethics—like every other facet of business—is a rapidly moving target...a race without a finish line. As good as any of us might think we are today, we have to be even better tomorrow and not just by a little, but by a lot."

---

[2]The material we received from Mr. Rust for this chapter is based on a speech he gave to the Association to Advance Collegiate Schools of Business-International (AACSB) in April 2005. Other remarks by Mr. Rust are included in Chapter 6.
[3]Her speech was delivered on April 12, 2005 and made available to us shortly thereafter. Parts of the speech were presented in earlier chapters.

She spoke about what Xerox is doing today under the umbrella of business ethics and social responsibility and why Xerox believes good practices in social responsibility helped save the company during the worst crisis in its history. Her talk concludes on the topic of "why what we are doing today seems so inadequate as we look to the future."

"I saw a statistic recently that about 50 global companies are larger than the economies of all but a dozen or so countries. And when you throw in the impact of the supplier base that these companies spawn and support, the results are even more startling," she explained. "With that economic might come awesome responsibilities. All of us need to ratchet up our expectations of what we can do collectively. I certainly don't have all the answers. I'm not even sure I have the right questions. But we are trying to push ourselves to think beyond the narrow limits of 'what is' and ask the tough questions about 'what if.'

"I know we can't solve the world's most pressing problems overnight, no more than we can eradicate hunger or illiteracy or nuclear proliferation or any of the dozens of other great challenges that confront us," she remarked. "But I know too that we must try. And so I'll end this talk where I began—by citing the wisdom of our founder Joe Wilson. He was an amazingly literate man who quoted Plato and Shakespeare with ease. Here's one of his favorites. It's from Robert Browning. To spare you my attempt at Elizabethan English, I'll paraphrase it:

> One man seeks a little thing to do, sees it, and does it. He keeps adding one by one and soon he hits a hundred.
>
> Another man pursues great dreams. He aspires to a million, dies before he reaches it, but misses by just a little.

"That strikes me as wise counsel," Mulcahy concluded. "I know that all of you who are connected to the Center for Business Ethics share that philosophy. You're all reaching for the stars. Even if you miss, you will still have made a quantum leap forward."

Mulcahy conveys a sense of momentum. Organizations must take a collective leap forward. They must stretch their expectations and extend their endeavors to the world's most pressing problems. Ethics-related initiatives must go beyond that which a CEO or business professional can evoke in a single individual and a single company.

This exclusive look into each CEO's approach shows that ethical initiatives must be interconnected among organizations. Not only does ethics need to be "transmitted" to the individual but each individual must acknowledge that their efforts are part of a tightly woven collective effort on an organizational and societal level. Ethics cannot be a solo effort. It requires a communion of efforts. Ethics must be embraced as more than a point-in-time requirement. It is a continuous approach—an entire mindset. Ethics on a societal level necessitates a unity of harmonized ethical initiatives across companies, across boundaries, and across time so that attention to ethics is constant, evolving, and widespread.

CEOs strive to ensure that ethical awareness is internalized by their employees and by the stakeholders external to their organizations. CEOs also confront the challenge of infusing others with the responsibility to uphold and build upon the organization's foundations, practices, and initiatives. Yes, inculcating these initiatives into individuals is important, but it is paramount to ensure that the individuals themselves feel they own the ethical process and progress.

Honesty, trust, integrity. Ethics is rooted in foundations and defining principles yet must be elastic enough to embrace changing contexts. The challenge is to make this mindset a part of every business professional's agenda. In one word: contagious.

Following the lead of Henry L. Meyer, CEO of KeyCorp, and drawing on the perspectives of the other CEOs, we ourselves might add:

Imagine a world:

Where ethics is contagious,
Where exemplary companies lead the way,
Where all companies strive to exceed legal requirements,
    ...with everyone building the momentum toward ethical excellence.

Index

Acknowledgments

MANY PEOPLE HAVE helped this book along the way. We owe a special thanks to our contributing CEOs for believing in our project when it was just an idea. Without their trust, this book would not have been possible. Communicating with them, their colleagues, and members of their staffs helped make the project come alive.

We have been privileged to have the guidance of Jeanne Glasser, Editorial Director at McGraw-Hill, every step of the way. Our appreciation also goes to Terry Deal, Editing Supervisor, and her team, for their assistance as our book went into production. Andy Winston was also helpful in the early part of the project.

We'd also like to acknowledge the support of our institutions: the College of Management of C.W. Post Campus of Long Island University and the Department of Economics, Business, and Statistics of the University of Milan (Università degli Studi di Milano).

We owe a special debt to Angela O'Neill, Secretary of the Department of Finance, C.W. Post Campus of Long Island University, for her skillful assistance, especially linking us while we were traveling and meeting in different time zones. We'd also like to thank our student assistants Vishal Patel, Wei-Na Wang, Anh Minh Le, Andrea M. Newman, and Trung Chi Nguyen, for their help with maintaining our project files at Long Island University.

Patrizia's personal thanks: My deepest gratitude to my mother, Vera Porrini, who never let me forget the heights I could reach.

A special thanks to my husband, John Fernandez, for his unwavering support and constant encouragement, especially during this project and, of course, to my little Giovanni Luca. Finally, thanks to my family and dear friends.

Lorene's personal thanks: Words alone can never express how grateful I am to my husband, Hermann Hiris, for his unwavering and unselfish understanding each and every day during the course of our project.

Gina's personal thanks: I'd like to acknowledge the support of my late husband, Tarcisio Mattei. Heartfelt thanks go to my family—to my brother Tom and his wife Denise, to my sister Janet and her husband Keith, and to the youngest of "the three sisters," Marie—for their constant support across the miles, and to the friends who were there for me, especially during the last year of the project. A special note of appreciation goes to Sue Cantoni, for her support and encouragement.

Finally, we are grateful to each other for bringing out our special gifts and for making the process a great journey of learning and friendship. Our conversations together allowed each of us to gain new perspectives, refine our thoughts, and weave new ideas into the tapestry of this work.

About the Authors

Patrizia Porrini, Ph.D., is Associate Professor of Management in the College of Management at the C.W. Post Campus of Long Island University. She earned her Ph.D. in Management at New York University, Stern School of Business, along with an M.Ph. in Statistics and an MBA in Finance, Management and International Business. She teaches management, negotiation, strategy, and organizational behavior. She is the recipient of numerous academic, research, and teaching awards, among them the Recognition Award for Excellence in Teaching, the Beta Gamma Sigma Outstanding Professor of the Year Award, and the Eastern Academy of Management Best Empirical Paper Award. Her research focuses on mergers and acquisitions, strategic alliances, negotiations, and firm performance. Her work has been published in *Journal of Management, Journal of High Technology Management Research, Journal of Business Research, Journal of Comparative and International Management,* and *International Encyclopaedia of the Social and Behavioral Sciences.* She has also presented papers and published proceedings at numerous national and international conferences and has served as editorial reviewer for conferences, academic journals, and publishers. During the past several years Patrizia has served on the undergraduate curriculum committee, where she has helped implement ethics-focused initiatives across all courses.

Lorene Hiris, D.P.S., is Professor of Finance in the College of Management at the C.W. Post Campus of Long Island University, where she teaches courses in managerial and international finance, both on campus and at the corporate headquarters in university-affiliated MBA programs. She is a recipient of the Newton Award for Teaching Excellence, the highest award LIU bestows for teaching. She has also served as Chair of the Department of Finance and she currently serves on the Advisory Board of YogaFit Training Systems Worldwide, Inc. She is regularly invited to teach at the Vienna University of Business and Economics and at Franklin College Switzerland. Her research affiliation as Senior Research Scholar is with the Economic Cycle Research Institute (ECRI) where she has contributed to their publications, *U.S. Cyclical Outlook* and *International Cyclical Outlook*. Her articles have been published in the *International Journal of Forecasting, International Review of Financial Analysis*, and *Research Strategies*, and as book chapters and proceedings. Her current research efforts are focused on ethics education and in delivering ethics across the curriculum. She is coauthor with Gina Poncini of conference papers and a book chapter analyzing CEO letters accompanying annual reports, comparing their treatment of ethics, scandals, and corporate governance before and after the passage of the Sarbanes-Oxley Act.

Gina Poncini, Ph.D., is Associate Professor in the Department of Economics, Business, and Statistics at the University of Milan. She teaches English Business Communication in the European Economics degree program and Political Communication in English in the graduate and undergraduate programs in political science and government. She also teaches Organizational Communication at NYU in Florence, Italy (Stern School of Business), and has taught communication-related seminars at the University of Lugano, Switzerland. Her research focuses on business meetings, intercultural business communication, financial communication, corporate responsibility, and communication in the agro-food industries, in particular the wine industry. Her in-depth analysis of international meetings is reported in the book *Discursive Strategies in Multicultural Business Meetings* (2004, 2007), which has been awarded as Distinguished Publication on Business Communication by the Association for Business Communication. She has coauthored papers with Lorene Hiris analyzing how ethics-related issues are addressed in CEO letters to shareholders—a project they began in 2003. Her articles have appeared in *Business Communication Quarterly*, *International Review of Applied Linguistics*, *Journal of Intercultural Studies*, and *Journal of Asian Pacific Communication*. She is currently serving a second term as Vice President Europe of the Association for Business Communication, and she has managerial experience in the international banking sector.